To the Hively Avenue Preschool
for happy learning
with clay

P. Helen Lewis

Oct. 27, 1988

American University Studies

Series XIV

Education

Vol. 9

PETER LANG

New York · Bern · Frankfurt am Main · Paris

Sara Smilansky,
Judith Hagan, Helen Lewis

Clay in the Classroom:

Helping Children Develop Cognitive
and Affective Skills for Learning

Foreword by Elliot W. Eisner

PETER LANG
New York · Bern · Frankfurt am Main · Paris

Library of Congress Cataloging-in-Publication Data

Smilansky, Sara:
  Clay in the classroom.
  (American university studies. Series XIV,
Education; vol. 9)
    Bibliography: p.
    Includes index.
    1. Modeling.   2. Child development.   3. Cognition
in children.   4. Learning.   I. Lewis, Helen, 1930-
II. Hagan, Judith.   III. Title.   IV. Series.
  LB1544.H34   1988   372.5'3   87-34243
  ISBN 0-8204-0354-7
  ISSN 0740-4565

CIP-Titelaufnahme der Deutschen Bibliothek

Smilansky, Sara:
Clay in the classroom : helping children develop cognitive and
affective skills for learning / Judith Hagan; Helen Lewis; Sara
Smilansky. Foreword by Elliot W. Eisner.– New York; Bern;
Frankfurt am Main; Paris: Lang, 1988
    (American university studies: Ser. 14, Education; Vol. 9)
    ISBN 0-8204-0354-7
NE: Lewis, Helen:; Hagan, Judith:; American university studies / 14

Printed by Weihert-Druck GmbH, Darmstadt (West Germany)

To Frank Maraffa, an ideal educator.

This book is dedicated to Frank Maraffa,
who was director of the Clay Project
for the Columbus Public Schools.
Through his efforts, the climate
necessary for such a complex and
challenging project to succeed was
made possible.

Acknowledgements

The clay research project was a field-based experiment of such proportions that it could not have been accomplished without the assistance and goodwill of literally hundreds of people. Its magnitude precludes our naming every person who contributed to the research and to making this book possible. It is a synergistic result of all their efforts. Most of them are mentioned in the text, the hundreds of children in Israel and in Columbus, Ohio, the classroom teachers, principals, custodians, secretaries, central office administrators, parents and the Community Communication Council were all part of the gigantic team who helped us learn how clay can be used in real classrooms to help real children improve their skills of learning. Wherever they are by this time in their lives we want to give them special thanks.

To others who contributed in special ways to the research we want to express our gratitude specifically. Charlotte Huddle worked as the on-site coordinator for Phase I of the project. She made difficult decisions and kept the project afloat when we were tempted to give up. Dr. Ross Mooney, gave invaluable theoretical insight into children's learning process and guidance from his wealth of experience with creative research. Vincent Vallese, then a graduate student, volunteered hours of his time in cleaning up computer data. Dr. Judith Bechtel, head of Freshman English at Northern Kentucky University, read our manuscript critically and advised us in writing and editting. Dr. Susan Hood, fine arts professor at Indiana University at South Bend, reviewed the text from the perspective of an art educator and journal editor. Dr. Elliot Eisner, author, art education authority and professor at Stanford University, graciously consented to review the final manuscript and to write the Foreword. All of them and Jay Wilson of Peter Lang Publishing Company have been most encouraging as we have struggled with the publishing process.

We thank all our friends, who have urged us to write this book, for their moral support. For the contents of the book and whatever deficencies and imperfections are therein, the authors are responsible.

We hope, with all those who had enough faith in a strange idea to give so much of themselves for it, that this book will enable the children in the readers' homes and classrooms to have the opportunity to learn joyfully with clay in their hands!

Judith Hagan
Helen Lewis
Sara Smilansky

Table of Contents

Foreword

The usual conception of the role of the arts in education is one that relegates them to matters of feeling, emotional release, and to play rather than as a fundamental resource for the educational development of the young. The visual arts and the uses of clay in the classroom, in particular, have been regarded as casual or incidental to the child's intellectual growth. After all, what could be educationally significant about making pinch-pots, imaginary animals, houses or people out of clay? Next to basket-weaving, the perennial whipping boy of the arts, clay is often regarded as a mindless medium that is intended to satisfy tactile needs, to provide diversion from the tough mental demands of the so-called solid subjects, and to keep children occupied on rainy afternoons.

Clay in the Classroom provides an entirely different view of the educational significance of clay. Sara Smilansky, Judith Hagan, and Helen Lewis have collaborated to provide an important study of the contributions that the use of clay can make to young children. Drawing upon their backgrounds in psychology and education, they have helped us understand clay's potential for increasing a wide range of intellectual skills, including those skills employed in the creation of clay forms.

We often take for granted the demands that clay can make upon the child. It is, after all, a very forgiving medium. A form that is unattractive can be reduced to a ball or a snake with little difficulty. One can easily begin again without waste of material. There are no codified rules either to break or to obey. Indeed, clay affords children a seemingly endless array of options that they can use and, in addition, they can make what they like in their own way.

To some observers, a task having such characteristics is "easy". What is often overlooked, is that to make something well — by whatever standards the child chooses to use — requires the child to compare, predict, control, plan, and appraise what he or she has done or is doing. Such forms of thinking, as Smilansky, Hagan, and Lewis have shown, are not only of consequence in the creation of successful clay forms. The mental skills that are elicited and developed through such tasks transfer to other areas of human performance as well. Many of these are those typically regarded as important educational outcomes. In short, the use of clay, particularly when children are given some guidance in technical matters, can have important intellectual as well as aesthetic or artistic consequences for children. Learning to think is fostered when the tasks even pre-school and kindergarten children engage in provide them with opportunities to think. Clay, the authors have shown us in a well-designed empirical study, provides such opportunities in abundance.

So much of the school curriculum, particularly at present, is of a rule-governed nature. The so-called "basics" that are so highly touted by those who wish to return schooling to the glories of yesterday provides students with very little scope for imagination to operate. (The last thing teachers want in their classrooms are creative spellers.) Even early arithmetic and reading as they are typically taught, do not provide children with much opportunity to exercise higher levels of cognition. Clay – a simple, ancient, and earthy material – when well taught does.

The phrase "when well taught" is critical. Any material can be reduced to conceptual rubble if not well taught. Indeed, the control group in the study reported in this volume did not fare at all well. Teachers can make a difference and Smilansky, Hagan, and Lewis have helped us understand how. This volume represents one of the relatively few efforts to base an approach to art teaching on a well developed empirical study. In that sense, the authors have provided a great service, not only to those professionally concerned with the advancement of art education, but even more important, to the children that art education is intended to serve.

Elliot W. Eisner
Stanford University

November, 1985

10

Preface

Clay is a medium often regarded as an "extra" or playtime type of material. *Clay in the Classroom* sets forth the reasons for going beyond this superficial understanding of clay to the realization that clay can become a learning tool for children. The foundation of this approach is a series of research studies conducted in the United States and Israel. These studies clearly indicate that arts activities, when provided in ongoing, structured programs, can assist children in improving their cognitive and affective skills.

The book begins with a foreword by Elliot Eisner, internationally recognized as a writer and innovator in the fields of art education and education. The foreword and a brief introduction provide the springboard for the unusual approach taken by the authors of this book: that it is possible to assist children to gain both cognitve and affective skills through the medium of clay.

Chapter One explains how the characteristics of clay give it potential to become a tool for learning in the classroom. The importance of nonverbal media in the educational setting is also discussed. In the next three chapters, the research study which came to be known as the Clay Project is described. Because of the unique characteristics of the Clay Project, it is of particular interest to teachers, administrators, parents, preschool staffs, and those in teacher-training institutions. From the beginning, classroom teachers were involved in all phases of the Clay Project, including deciding what questions needed to be asked and the procedures to be used to find the answers. The Clay Project took three years to complete, and during the year in which three teaching strategies using clay were implemented, 27 schools with 53 classrooms and approximately 1,600 children were involved. Findings of the American study, since it was based on a prior research done in Israel, have cross-cultural implications.

Since the Clay Project was completed, hundreds of additional children have been exposed to clay as a learning tool in the classroom setting, from the Midwest of America to Hong Kong! Chapter

11

Five looks at a number of the children who have experienced clay in the classroom in a variety of schools, and describes the impact of clay activities on cognitive, physical, social, and emotional growth. The practicalities of using clay in the classroom are dealt with in Chapter Six, including how to acquire the best type of clay and prepare it for use, and suggestions for distributing, collecting and storing clay. Sample clay lessons are also included.

Chapter Seven is a brief but important discussion about the need to balance current trends in early childhood education, especially those which focus primarily on cognitively based activities, with experiences which allow children to explore and learn in other ways as well. If children are to reach their full potential, they must be given the time to acquire the emotional, physical and creative skills necessary to make sense of the world and to survive the demands of living in a computer age. Ironically, one of the most ancient of mediums, clay, may provide us with one of the tools which can help children prepare to meet the challenges of the 21st century.

Skillbuilding

Look at the faces of these children
And then look at what they have done
Which creates such looks upon these faces.

These are very young children, four and five,
And they have been learning how to work with clay.
Please note: I said learning.
Someone, a caring, understanding and trained adult,
Has interacted with these children and helped them
Understand that in the world are substances
Which can be transformed into other shapes
Resembling reality real or imagined.
However, that transformation doesn't happen
Just because you wish it so; it must be coaxed
And assisted into being, and the skill
To make this happen can be taught.

What makes this teaching of skills more challenging
Is that each child already has developed certain skills,
And no two children are exactly at the same developmental level.
So you can teach for generalization
But you intervene with each child specifically.
It is necessary for learning, however,
To discover what skills and understandings
The individual child already owns
Before attempting to help him own others.
Along with this, understand it is not
In books or diagrams or little sheets alone
That learning can take place; try a piece of
Soft earth clay, which, when used for more
Than therapy or expressions or muscle building
Can become a tool for exploration, idea building,
Planning, generalization, categorizing,
Concept clarifying, interpretation, evaluating,
Interrelating, discovering, studying.

Then look again at the faces
Which say to us who think we are in control,
"We are ready to learn. Will you help us?"

And then make that learning so enjoyable
It doesn't need sugar coating or a make-up job,
Or, later on, plastic surgery.

— Judith Hagan

INTRODUCTION

Clay in the classroom? What is significant about that? Clay is fine for children as a free time activity choice or as a reward for good behavior, but it certainly isn't a material which will contribute directly to a child's development or learning . . . or is it?

Intensive research during the past decade has sought ways to improve the performance of children in the classroom setting. Many solutions have been proposed and implemented in the early childhood education area. Many of these were particularly targeted for the more disadvantaged children. Often, remedies for the lack of readiness expect young students to build upon skills, social or verbal, which are either lacking or weak. Some skills and interests which many young children do have are often ignored or poorly utilized by researchers. In turn, many early childhood educators are unaware of potential avenues to helping children learn.

One researcher who has studied hundreds of children, both in the United States and Israel, utilizing the classroom as a research site, is Dr. Sara Smilansky. From her earliest work in the area of play, later drawing, and most recently clay, Smilansky has examined ways in which the areas of strength and the interests of young children can become springboards to learning. Each carefully constructed study has clearly indicated significant growth, cognitive as well as affective, occurs in children exposed to instruction in such areas as drawing and clay modeling.

In 1968, Smilansky's book *The Effects of Sociodramatic Play*, gave the results of a pioneering research into the importance of play to the young child. Smilansky's study gave empirical evidence that teachers can intervene in order to help young children develop play skills. For many early childhood educators in both Israel and the United States, it was a book which was a revelation, resulting in many further studies and curriculum revisions.

What was there about play which demanded attention? Smilansky discovered that children who did well in school were also able to engage in higher levels of sociodramatic play. In addition, play activities could be directly tied to the child's own interests and particular background. Play did not require children to depend upon the weakest of their skills, those in the cognitive areas. Instead, as the research demonstrated, these weaker cognitive skills could be strength-

16

ened through the play activities carefully planned and structured by the teacher.

From play, Smilansky moved to another medium of expression natural to young children, drawing. In the late sixties, Tel-Aviv University and the Tel-Aviv public schools became collaborators with The Ohio State University and the Columbus, Ohio public schools. Classroom teachers, art teachers, Title I supervisors, researchers and a variety of administrators became partners in designing and implementing the research. The classroom itself became the research laboratory. Judith Hagan, an art teacher in the Columbus schools, joined the research team and worked directly with preschool children and their teachers. Hagan also assisted in the pre and post testing and later in the evaluation of the data.

The results of the drawing research were published in 1973 in a final report (*An Experiment in the Use of Drawing to Promote Cognitive Development in Disadvantaged Preschool Children in Israel and the United State*). This research used a wide range of testing materials, five treatment groups, and pre and post-testing of 140 children from Israel and the United States. An increase in IQ of an average of 16 points was indicated after structured drawing activities lasting ten weeks. Cognitive and affective growth were found to be closely intertwined, and could be effectively combined by classroom teachers to help children increase a variety of skills.

The knowledge and experience gained from the play and drawing projects provided a firm foundation for another research study done in Israel and the United States. Again, under Smilansky's direction, the classroom became the research base of operations, but this time clay was the medium utilized. Children in both Tel-Aviv and Columbus prekindergarten and kindergarten classes used clay for 16 weeks as part of planned school activities. Four teaching methods or strategies were studied to discover which would best enable children to grow both artistically and cognitively. From the initial stages, teachers were partners in designing, implementing, and evaluating the study. Dr. Helen Lewis, whose area of expertise is the language of the young child, took leave from her position at Indiana University at South Bend to become director of the three-year project. Lewis also was responsible for facilitating one of the four teaching strategies, called the Observation/Discussion Group. Judith Hagan, who earlier had worked with Smilansky on the drawing research, became a fulltime staff member, acting as art coordinator for the clay project and as leader of the Technique Group. The third fulltime staff member, Charlotte Huddle, was a Columbus Public Schools' guidance counselor at the elementary school level; she was in charge of the Encouragement Group. The fourth group was the Control Group. Lewis, Hagan, and Huddle, together with Smilansky as a consultant, were the coordinators of the clay project, but the classroom teachers did the actual implementing of the methods in their individual classrooms: 53 classrooms and about 1600 children.

What does clay offer to children as a medium of expression and as a means of learning? In drawing, three-dimensional concepts are communicated in two-dimensional ways. Thus, children must change objects they are viewing into flat, usually linear interpretations before they can be drawn on a piece of paper. When working with clay, children can view the world around them, then transfer an observation which is meaningful to them directly to the clay as a three-dimensional interpretation. For children who are less experienced at intellectual problem solving and who have little experience with drawing, working with clay can be less frustrating. Clay allows for flexibility without the penalties associated with paper/pencil or crayon activities. With clay, erasing is done by smoothing out the clay or reshaping parts; changing ideas is possible and encouraged by the flexibility of the medium.

In order to discover how well children were able to communicate through the clay medium, and if communication skills transferred into other areas, the research study also looked at language development and at drawing abilities. In addition to several tests available commercially, others were developed by the staff of the clay project. These tests were used by classroom teachers and the staff to look at how children changed during the 16 week period of working with clay. (See Appendix)

Despite the differences in cultures, the children who participated in the Israeli research and the children in the United States project showed very similar results. The combined experimental teaching method groups, Encouragement, Observation/Discussion, and Technique, made significantly more improvements in clay, drawing, and language development when compared to the control group. The technique teaching method proved to be the most effective for the majority of the preschoolers in the project. This was true whether or not the children scored high, medium, or low in intellectual ability, classroom adjustment, sculptural ability, and verbal skills. A further significant discovery was how effective clay is as a medium for development, particularly of boys who begin preschool less prepared and experienced for the schooling process.

Since the study was completed, staff members have continued to conduct seminars, workshops, classes and other types of approaches to promote the use of clay in the classroom. Further opportunities to observe the impact of planned programs with clay activities on both teachers and students has reinforced the validity of the study. It is particularly important in this time of the so-called "back to the basics" movement and the rush to enter the computer revolution that educators not lose sight of the need children have for both affective and cognitive learning. While millions of dollars can be spent on high technology for the classroom and updated textbooks, without the inner resources and motivation required to utilize these children will be unable to make sense out of what is being demanded of them. What is needed is a balanced approach, one which allows children the chance to discover who they are as well as what the world expects of them.

For early childhood educators, the implications of the study are clear: Here is a medium — clay — often overlooked, frequently dismissed as too messy for the classroom setting (it doesn't need to be, as Chapter Six explains!), but which, when used in a structured program, can contribute directly to the preschool-aged child's development of learning skills. Clay can help the young child better understand his or her world by allowing for the acquisition of concepts which are relatively abstract despite the concrete qualities of the medium. Children are also able to transfer what they have learned from the clay medium into other areas such as language. The significance of cross-cultural application makes the use of clay in the classroom to promote learning important across barriers of national boundaries as well.

Here, in one of humankind's oldest mediums of expression, is a way in which many children can be helped to learn. Clay, found in the earth, shaped and molded by young hands, also helps to shape and mold the mind, allowing the young child an additional way in which to discover and make sense of the world.

1

CLAY: WHO NEEDS IT?

Characteristics of Clay

Clay is one of mankind's oldest art media. For members of the earliest cultures, clay was important for more than its artistic potential. Objects used in everyday life such as the vessels utilized as containers for a variety of materials, from water to grain, were made from this substance found in the earth. The bits and pieces of such vessels, called shards, help archeologists determine the age as well as the social, artistic and religious aspects of particular cultures. Many of the clay pieces and other ceramic works now in museums had a functional importance long before museum curators gathered them as works of art for display.

Even today, in our high technological society, there is something vital and exciting about working with clay. Present almost anyone of any age with a moist ball of clay and there is an almost spontaneous leap into a world of creation. Hands and fingers explore the texture, the flexibility and malleability of the medium. Ideas emerge and reemerge easily, with no penalties for change and exploration. Whether ideas come from observation of reality or are from the imagination, clay adapts to a wide range of concepts in many different ways.

Perhaps the enjoyment expressed by most children when given the opportunity to work in clay is the reason why teachers often use it for rewards or for "special occasions." But clay, found in the earth and part of a long heritage shared by all, is much more than a material to be used for brief moments when busy schedules can be altered, or when there is nothing else to do. Particularly for young children, clay can help make sense of an often bewildering world. Clay can assist children in developing concepts, communicating ideas and finding methods of self-expression.

It is important to recognize that the kind of clay used can have a great impact upon the experience. Substitutes for clay, such as plasticene and dough-like types, do not offer the range of qualities and characteristics found in the earth clays. There are several factors which make earth clay a better choice, including the responsiveness of the medium, the manageability, and the cost. These will be discussed in detail later in this chapter, and in Chapter Six.

Psychologists and clinicians, particularly those faithful to psychoanalytic theories, emphasize the cathartic and sublimative value of working in clay; they see it as primarily a means of release from aggressive drives, as well as an acceptable way of expressing curiosity about anal and sexual objects. They tend to emphasize the aspect of emotional release, regarding clay as a good projective material for diagnosing emotional and developmental conditions (Hartley et al, 1964; Smilansky, 1971; Wollheim, 1974).

Hartley and his colleagues stress, among other things, the social value of working with clay. Since this activity is often done in groups, it can serve as a means for creating a social bond, particularly for the restrained or fearful child. Making things with clay can serve as a protective coat behind which hesitant children can get to know their classmates. A table of children all at work making objects from clay seem to feel part of a group effort, and social pressure is lessened or nonexistent. Observers of children engaged in clay activities notice how free-flowing their speech is and how many references are made to events or images from the children's world.

One of the century's outstanding art educators, Victor Lowenfeld, was interested in the intellectual aspects of creativity. In his book *Creative and Mental Growth* (1957), Lowenfeld noted the sensory-motoric aspects of clay modeling activities, particularly at nursery school ages of two to six years. The development of artistic and intellectual abilities in the preschematic stage, ages five to seven, were analyzed, and it was noted that at this stage the search for ways in which to shape the clay to give it definite form had emerged. Clay, according to Lowenfeld, is an invaluable aide in awakening thinking of a new type. The three-dimensionality and plasticity of clay adapt to the flexibility of the concepts being discovered and internalized by the young child: "through the plasticity of clay the child has an easier means of deviating from his concept than in other mediums. In building up the figure, the child actually has the opportunity for accompanying it kinetically in some imaginary experiences." Lowenfeld also pointed out the importance of activity in clay to the development of children's sense of personal value and self-worth.

Compared to other artistic media such as those used in drawing, clay has received relatively little investigation by researchers and educators in child development. The medium of clay may seem to present to researchers problems with such aspects as management and storage. Just as it appears to many classroom teachers easier to provide pencils and crayons and paper than clay for those students in their classroom, so it may seem simpler to those studying art media to do the same. Opportunities to do longterm projects using clay quickly convince most teachers and researchers that storage and manageability obstacles can be overcome. For example, researchers can photograph clay pieces for later study, saving enough sample pieces to clarify certain aspects. Familiarity with clay and how it can be used in a classroom setting creates an awareness of the rewards which far outweigh liabilities. Both teachers and researchers need to spend time observing and understanding the benefits to children which come from working in the medium of clay. Growth in cognitive as well as affective areas can occur when clay becomes part of the ongoing process of learning in the classroom.

What does happen to children who engage in clay activities over a period of time in a planned program? Modeling with clay helps develop both small and large muscles. Hand and eye coordination can be improved even as children satisfy a need for sensory stimulation. Awareness of such areas as texture, shape, size, and space become better understood as the clay is formed, pressed, smoothed, roughened, indented, etc. Imaginative play with clay is natural for children at all ages, and the opportunity to use imagination is an important aspect of learning for children.

Three basic characteristics of clay, its three-dimensionality, flexibility, and manipulative qualities, allow children to actually think through the medium itself. Children are able to grow in cognitive ways through a medium usually considered only appropriate for affective or artistic expression. Looking further at the three characteristics, each can be understood in relation to the cognitive as well as affective growth of individual children:

Three-dimensionality: the child considers a number of dimensions at once. Observations and perceptions are broadened.

24

One-sided judgments are made more difficult, and children are encouraged to try to integrate varying observations.

Flexibility: clay facilitates "trying out" ideas, allows for continuous change, and provides children with a sense of freedom of both action and choice.

Manipulation: recognized by most educators and researchers, particularly by Piagetians, as basic to the development of logical thinking and language. Without manipulative activities, children have difficulty or cannot progress to higher levels of thinking. During clay activities, stages of growth in manipulation can be observed beginning with pounding and flattening and progressing to the shaping of realistic, upright figures.

When a child attempts to create a representation of something observed in the "real" world, it is the concept of that object, event, or subject which is the basis of the creation. For example, each child has acquired a concept of dog from various experiences with a variety of dogs. If children are asked to make a dog, each child goes through a process of screening from all dogs what constitutes "dogness" or the basic concept of dog. The process of generalizing unifies separate experiences and produces classifications which make abstractions and generalization possible.

In performing the transaction, working from incoming forms to outgoing forms, from past experiences to present ones, each child has a way of affecting the world. Comparing the concept of dog (internal) to the perception of the dog being created in the clay (external) is a cognitive process. An affective process occurs out of the act of creation itself as expression of feelings and emotions. At the end of the process, there is an integral form that has been created to express the concept.

Working in clay also offers children the opportunity to develop concepts of dimensions such as size, shape, and quantity. These dimensions involve locating an object and its parts in space; comparing an object and its parts in terms of size, shape, and importance; and evaluating an object and its parts regarding such aspects as whether something stands or falls, is right or wrong, fits or doesn't fit. Even young children can begin to understand such concepts as here-there, in-out, high-low, bigger-smaller, wetter-dryer, rounder-flatter, same-different, through activity in clay. Teachers can help each child discover through clay what these words actually mean rather than trying to explain or demonstrate them to a class. Through interactions with the clay, the process of learning can be made both enjoyable and meaningful. When the young child is involved in clay activities, the level of openness for cognitive skill building increases. The teacher who is aware of this and prepared to capitalize upon the opportunity will be amazed at the results.

Advantages of Non-Verbal Media

> The current literature on disadvantaged children indicates that they learn best in more concrete, inductive, kinesthetic and less verbal situations. In view of this, teachers should search for methodology coordinated with this learning style.
> (Fantini and Weinstein, 1969)

Because of the importance of verbal and language performance in cognitive development, virtually all existing programs used to foster cognitive growth in young children are based primarily on verbalization and language skills. Yet numerous studies (Bernstein, 1962; Goldstein, 1967; Deutsch, 1968) show that verbal and language performance of many young children, particularly those from lower socio-economic backgrounds, is relatively low. In actuality, most programs try to help children overcome their cognitive weaknesses by expecting children to use those very skills in which they are often the poorest: language and verbalization.

For many teachers, learning to work with children whose backgrounds and frames of reference are far different from their own is difficult and frustrating. In order to understand fully the language of young children of any background, the context for that language must be recognized.

The context influences language in many complex, subtle and pervasive ways. It not only affects *how* children talk in regard to dialect variations and registers, but also *when* and *for* what purposes they use language. Many of the problems children from minority cultures face in school can be traced to misunderstanding and value conflict in regard to communication.

(King, 1975)

The transition from one context for language to another is challenging for both teachers and students. In order to assist young children in understanding cognitive aspects of the educational process that exists in school systems, the teacher must present the child with the context within which that cognitive learning, and the language to understand it, can be developed. "The teacher creates a climate for learning that offers opportunities to children with diverse interests and competencies, that accepts and respects whatever language they bring, and that fosters human relationships – and language – through engagement in meaningful work." (King, 1975)

Beyond the challenge to help children from widely differing backgrounds share the common language of school, there is the need for making certain children understand the meaning of words which makeup that language.

What we must remember about words is that they are like freight cars; they may carry a cargo of meaning, of associated, nonverbal reality, or they may not. The words that enter our minds with a cargo of meaning make more complete and accurate our nonverbal model of the universe. Other words just rattle around in our heads. We may be able to spit them out, or shuffle them around according to rules, but they have not changed what we really know and understand about things. One of the things that is so wrong with school is that most of the words children hear there carry no nonverbal meaning whatsoever, and so add nothing to their real understanding. Instead, they only confuse them, or worse yet, encourage them to feel that if they can talk glibly about something, it means that they understand it.

(Holt, 1969)

Particularly for young children, it is important to provide activities during which words can take on meaning and become part of each child's understanding. What King calls meaningful work is another way of describing this providing of activities. Each activity or experience should be based upon the needs and interests of particular age groups or individual children. By discovering where children are in regard to their strengths and weaknesses, teachers can do much more to enable them to turn the weaknesses into strengths. One strength shared by many children is a strong interest in materials which can be manipulated. Hands-on activities of many types appeal to children. This is particularly true if the activities are well-organized and at the same time allow for flexibility and spontaneity. Non-verbal media such as drawing and clay are excellent examples of materials which lend themselves to such hands-on experiences. Clay especially appeals to many children due to its tactile and kinesthetic aspects. Through a variety of planned experiences with such media, children can learn to respond to the world of school in more positive and meaningful ways. The context for learning becomes one of discovery through manipulation of materials such as clay, which is nonthreatening and enjoyable. Ideas become real in ways not possible with just words: "bigger" is a better understood concept when a small clay animal is compared with one much larger; "inside" assumes more meaning when a bowl has been shaped from the clay so that the outside wall of clay holds the inside shape. Most children love to experiment, and with clay such experimentation can result in better comprehension of many ideas and concepts. Many aspects of a single idea can be examined, and even at a young age children can grasp the idea of solving a problem in many different ways.

Children who learn a concept by means of a nonverbal medium, and can express that concept in that particular medium, will then, with relative ease, translate that knowledge and use it in verbal expression. A concept needs to be understood before it can be correctly expressed. Children must internalize or "own" a concept, which can then be expressed nonverbally, and, finally, verbally. It is the knowing that he or she knows which is vital to the internalization and assimilation of concepts into the child's system of learning. For many children, bypassing the process of manipulation activities which offer a range of nonverbal learning segments, can mean never fully comprehending the language of schools and therefore of a large segment of society. While this manipulative learning is particularly

28

appropriate and important for younger ages of children (preschool and early primary), it is also helpful and sometimes vital to the learning of older children as well.

The use of a medium such as clay cannot replace verbal methods of learning and teaching. However, it can be an *additional* method which, when used in a structured program, can provide access for many children to the learning process. In the preschool and the elementary school settings, where verbal and writing skills tend to dominate (particularly in the past decade), nonverbal media often are ignored or overlooked. Research described in other chapters of this book clearly indicates that a nonverbal medium such as clay may make the difference between discovering school as a place to learn and school as a place in which to become frustrated and bored.

Learning through Diversified Media

Utilizing a variety of media, some verbal and some nonverbal, can better serve the needs of young children. Conceiving an object or concept through several types of media allows children to focus on different aspects of the same idea. Drawing an object, making it with clay and writing a story about that object or idea would offer broader modes of perception and result in more flexible thought processes. Each kind of medium requires a unique perception and conception in order to express an idea. Drawing a person is a different process from making a person with clay; writing a story about a person or telling about a person calls upon different skills and methods in each case. If all of these ways of communicating "person" are built into the structure of the learning process, children have ways of reinforcing, expanding and developing the original concept of a person. That child who begins as less skilled in a certain area, such as verbalization, is not penalized but instead receives support through recognition of other valid ways of communicating ideas which the child may have. When teachers regard as equally important and correct the communication of an idea through any of the media, whether clay, drawing or words, then children may find school a much less threatening place, especially in the beginning years. After discovering success in one medium, there is more likelihood that children will feel confident enough to try other media as well.

Because the manipulative stage usually is regarded as a preliminary one to others, such as the analytical stage, does not mean that the manipulation of media is less important or lower in terms of abilities. What is indicated is that manipulation is vital and often needs to precede other ways of learning. Recent research on the brain hemispheric functions has revealed that many children do learn more easily and with deeper understanding if given the opportunity to use the right brain function involving spatial skills as well as the ability so see in wholes. For this type of learner, having to analyze and break ideas down into smaller and smaller parts can be frustrating, at least as an initial experience. Nonverbal media such as clay and drawing can provide these students having strong right brain learning patterns with ways to indicate their understanding of concepts and problems in different but equally valid ways as those from the left brain learning styles, which utilize the verbal and written language skills. Is it right to penalize those learners who are just as intelligent but who happen to have other approaches to solving problems or looking at the world?

Once a child has mastered communicating a concept or idea in one medium, that child may need help in order to transfer and then express that concept or idea in another medium. For example, the class may have learned to use the word "tall" to differentiate among people, trees, or houses of various heights. Children have learned to differentiate among a variety of objects in the environment and to express this knowledge verbally. But when they have to express the same knowledge through a drawing, they must make other differentiations among objects. The auditory form of "tall" is quite different from its visual form. The concept must be expressed both physically and abstracly. Standing next to another child and saying "I am taller" is not sufficient if the concept is to be expressed through drawing. This change in the medium of expression invites a new burst of cognitive and emotional growth.

This burst of growth can go beyond the realm of expression and increase the perceptual abilities of individual children. Finding themselves able to express knowledge about such aspects as position, size, brightness, and color, children discover variations of these characteristics within their environments. Each mode of expression has a related mode of perception. When the expression or perception grows, the other grows as well.

However, certain limitations to the transposition of knowledge among media and ways of expressing that knowledge need to be taken into account. Some knowledge cannot be transposed easily from one medium to another. It is doubtful if different senses and their correlated modes of expression would have evolved if any idea could be equally well expressed through any one avenue such as words, music, clay, or painting. Some ideas seem so perfectly stated in one media that transfering them to others would destroy the inherent quality of the original expression. But given the unique characteristics of each medium, many ideas can be revealed through a variety of media, each remaining true to the inherent quality of the particular mode, but still stating in different ways the same theme or idea.

In addition to the development of perceptual and conceptual skills, the use of both verbal and nonverbal media can enhance the self-concept of children. A clay piece or drawing is a tangible and visual sign for a child that he or she can create. This creation can then become a statement others may interpret and understand. Spoken words are not visible. The presence of concepts in visible form permits ready feedback to children which supports their "knowing they know." Progression in self-claimed learning is more readily provided to young children through evidence of ideas brought forth by means of a drawing or clay work. Confidence builds as children discover that this act of creation can be repeated, and that with each repetition new and additional aspects can be drawn or shaped. Particularly for children with poor self-images and a lack of experience in using their power to create, producing an art work may be an important method of developing self-confidence and a sense of self-worth. This may not mean placing emphasis upon the product as much as the process, especially for younger children. It is the act of creation which often brings a sense of power and control, and may for some children represent a rare opportunity to feel powerful and in control. Depriving children of experiences such as these through the act of creation does a disservice to them and to the entire learning process as well.

2

CLAY: RESEARCHING IT

Classroom Research

Teaching today is an occupation with a great many concerns and frustrations. Despite the importance of salaries, working conditions, seniority, etc., there are many teachers who continue to take time to discover ways in which they can better meet the needs of children in their classrooms. In order to learn what methods work best for which children, teachers must evaluate. This process of evaluation is one that is vital to what is often referred to as research. Research has come to hold a negative connotation for many teachers. This is unfortunate, because much of what concerned, motivated, and in-novative teachers do is, indeed, a form of research. Looking at a problem, discovering its components, trying out ways to solve either the entire problem or an aspect of it, and then evaluating the results: this is research. And in many schools, it goes on, in some form or another, all the time. It may not be scientific in its structure, or analytical in its approach, or even valid across groups in its results, but if there is a discovery of something that works, that makes a positive difference for children and teachers, then it is research and experimentation with meaning and purpose.

It is precisely this classroom type of research which Smilansky and the clay project team tried to utilize. While more scientific structure was applied, data analyzed, and evaluation procedures carefully planned, the over-riding mode was that of the classroom teacher eager to discover what does work for children in a school setting. For some of the many teachers who became part of the study, some of the process of experimentation and evaluation was at first uncomfortable or even threatening. But once the idea that this research was based upon the reality of the classroom became clear; that it was not an idea generated by people completely unrelated to what really goes on in schools; then teachers became, in all senses of the word, partners in the research. As individual teachers began to see what was happening to children participating in the study, the purpose and potential of the approaches became more meaning-ful. Evidence that "real" learning was occurring began to appear; a dynamic, exciting research partnership was paying off for both children and teachers. How this partnership was established is the topic of this chapter.

Asking the Questions

Based upon preliminary studies done in both Tel Aviv, Israel, and Columbus, Ohio, a number of questions emerged concerning the use of clay activities in preschool and primary classrooms. The Israeli project preceded the American study and established much of the groundwork. In Israel, fewer children and teachers were involved than would later participate in the American research project. The number in the sample was large enough, however, to indicate that there was a need and that major questions related to children and clay in the classroom should be answered. Smilansky found in Israel that there were great differences among classroom teachers regarding how often clay was used with students. Many variations also existed with respect to the amount of intervention and expectations of the teachers. The experience of the Israeli study relative to evaluation methods and styles of teacher intervention provided a foundation on which to build and adapt to meet the needs of the population to be served in Columbus.

The American study was a three year project which took place in a variety of school settings with the cooperation of many teachers and students. During the first part of the study, Phase One, children were observed and tested in order to establish procedures and set standards for the testing and interviewing to be used in the Phase Two, or research period. Children who participated in Phase One were from a wide range of backgrounds, including those from advantaged as well as disadvantaged environments. (See pages 41—45 for clarification of advantaged/disadvantaged descriptions). Private preschools as well as federally-funded ones were utilized in the sampling in order to provide a full range of responses and scores for the various testing and interviewing instruments. For example, it would be helpful to have evidence of how children who were slightly older as well as somewhat more experienced would perform. This would allow for growth in Phase Two children who scored exceptionally or even somewhat higher than normal. Therefore, children from preschool age to second grade were tested during the Phase One year.

All of the tests were carefully screened and evaluated regarding their application to young children. Those tests which had been used in the Israeli study were adjusted where necessary to avoid confusion in results because of cultural differences. (An example would be showing a picture of something peculiar to Israel but which be unfamiliar to an American child and expecting a verbal description of what the object is). Classrooms teachers participated from the first stages of the study, during Phase I, in the development of tests as well as their administration, scoring and evaluation. More complete descriptions of the tests used for the pre and posttesting are to be found in this chapter as well as in Chapter Four. Clay Project developed tests are included in the Appendix.

It was clear from the Israeli results that changes of a significant level could be gained by the use of clay in a structured program with young children, especially those from more disadvantaged backgrounds. Now the question remained: Would those findings hold true for American children as well? Although the basic thrust of the study done in Israel was carried into the American research, the larger number of participants and the longer time span enabled more complexity and depth in the American Clay Project. The three broad goals for what became known in Columbus as "the clay project" were similar to those previously established in Tel Aviv:

1. To identify teaching strategies for intervention in clay activities that would promote growth in verbal cognitive skills of prekindergarten and kindergarten aged children.
2. To train teachers and aides in teaching strategies using clay.
3. To develop and refine valid and reliable instruments for teachers use in measuring, evaluating, and monitoring children's levels or performance in working with clay and any changes in verbal cognitive performance.

Based upon the goals for the clay project, the preliminary research done in Israel, and the results of Phase One, specific questions were determined to have particuliar importance:

36

1. What is cognitive about clay sculpture?
2. What is artistic about clay sculpture?
3. Does teacher intervention in children's clay sculpturing foster cognitive development as well as artistic development?
4. Do children transfer what they have learned in clay activities to other artistic and cognitve tasks?
5. Does the strategy used in teaching clay activities make a difference in the development of children?
6. Which type of teaching strategy is best for which type of child according to age, sex, intelligence, social and emotional adjustment, and clay abilities of the child?

Strategies for Teaching

Although the primary focus of the study was what works best for children, as the questions asked indicate, teachers were also important elements to be considered. It would be unrealistic and unproductive to ask teachers to interact with children using strategies which were not suitable to classrooms with young children. Therefore, close attention was paid to what types of teacher interventions might be appropriate but at the same time provide information about how children could be assisted in the learning process.

No one best method of teacher intervention or way to have the children manipulate the medium of clay was assumed. If the artistic and cognitive development of *all* children in a particular classroom was considered, it was obvious that attempting to have a strategy that might work equally well in all cases was unrealistic. However, based upon the experience of the project staff as well as the work done in Israel and in Phase One, three teaching strategies were chosen: encouragement, observation and discussion, and technique. Within each strategy, ways to foster cognitive, artistic and verbal development were designed. The first two experimental methods, encouragement and observation/discussion, were based primarily upon the views of Victor Lowenfeld and his supporters. These views suggest that the stimulation, intervention, and guidance of children involved in art activities such as clay modeling should relate to emotional and intellectual spheres but should not have direct adult intervention in the children's work techniques. On the contrary, any technical guidance might impair the children's creative development. This approach to working with children while they are engaged in art activities is used particularly by persons with little art training, who often feel unqualified or unprepared to assist children with the more technical aspects of making art. Those who hold this view and have been educated as art teachers or artists frequently were trained during the period of time that Lowenfeld and his followers were the primary source of information and preparation for art education. While the focus of attention has changed somewhat over the past twenty years, the Lowenfeld philosophy still has validity for many people.

Another point of view, one which was the underlying one for the technique strategy, was that children need more than emotional and intellectual stimulation if they are to be successful in doing artwork and if they are to continue to grow and develop in their artistic abilities. In the technique approach, emotional and cognitive stimulation was combined with a certain amount of direct teaching and guidance in the techniques required to be successful in creating clay works. Young children face a number of technical problems in the creative process, some of which they are unable to solve on their own. Some children simply give up, others may try another solution which may or may not work, and a few keep at the problem until they work out an answer. It is possible that reversals or slowdowns in the developmental process can occur as the result of repeated failures, and that serious frustration can eventually cause some children to become negative about art experiences. Parallels can be found in how young children learn to read. Quite often, children who develop reading problems do so as the result of frustrating and negative experiences at the beginning levels. Of course, some problems occur due to a lack of readiness on the part of the child; but others are the result of teaching strategies which were inadequate or inappropriate for particular children. Whether in art or in reading, such situation can be particularly damaging to those children who have not developed an active will to confront difficulties. By providing children with information and advice about ways to solve specific problems they themselves recognize as problems, or by establishing

38

ways for children to avoid difficulties so that problems don't need to develop, teachers can help prevent much of the frustration and failure.

Each of these viewpoints, and the strategies for teaching designed to correlate with them, were regarded as equally valid for helping young children develop cognitively and affectively. No definite conclusions were held by the research team before the study as to which of the views or strategies might best fit children's needs. In training each group of teachers who formed each of the three experimental groups, the type of intervention was presented as probably being as the "best" by the research team in order to be certain that each method received the strongest possible support during the classroom trial period. During Phase Two, when teachers were utilizing one of the three strategies in their classrooms, it was vital the teachers believed that the particular method they were using was beneficial for most children.

The Encouragement Group was based on the rationale that children have the ability, and given the opportunity, would develop skill in clay activities on their own. Children in this group were provided time for clay sculpturing, necessary materials, ready approval for products created, and encouragement in all phases of the clay activity times. Teachers were given ideas to help them work with the children in nondirective ways. Vocabulary was extremely important, and much of the training period of the Encouragement Group teachers was spent on learning to say the right thing to a child at the right time. Teachers were not to assign subjects or objects to be made with the clay, nor were they to assist children with technical problems which might arise during clay activities. Children were expected to work with the clay as each chose to do so, within the guidelines of normal classroom behavior and proper management expectations (such as getting out and putting away materials). With the support and encouragement of the teacher, children would discover their own solutions to the problems which might occur, enjoying the process of working with the clay and moving through the various development levels at their own speed.

In the *Observation/Discussion Group*, teachers went beyond encouragement to provide visual and verbal stimulation. For this group, the rationale was that children have the ability to work with the clay and can solve technical problems that might occur, but need assistance with seeing their environment and in verbalizing ideas. If teachers could help children learn how to select and organize their memories of a subject through the process of discussion, then children could develop skills in sculpturing and language when asked to work with the clay. For this group, a series of subjects was established; these subjects or topics were based upon what seemed to interest children who worked with clay during the Phase One period. They were also subjects which were compatible with the clay medium itself, and would lend themselves to a full range of abilities and levels. Each subject was discussed by the teacher with the class, and whenever possible through direct observation and experience (such as a dog visiting the class just before dogs were to be made with clay). During training sessions, teachers in the Observation/Discussion Group brainstormed ideas about ways to present each topic to the children. As in the Encouragement Group, teachers were not to directly assist children who might encounter difficulties with clay techniques. Teachers could, however, use a questioning strategy to help children become aware of possible ways to analyze problems.

The Technique Group teachers used the rationale that children could develop in their ability to work with clay more effectively if technical assistance was made available. Also important was the encouragement of each child, and a range of observation and discussion opportunities related to each topic. As in the Observation/Discussion Group, there were set topics for 13 of the 16 weeks. Unlike the Encouragement and Observation Groups, the Technique Group was designed to help teachers find ways to assist children with the clay medium itself. Teachers drew attention to the nature and characteristics of the clay, showing how forms could be shaped and textures made using a variety of techniques. Advice and suggestions were provided concerning how to make parts of a clay piece stay together or to help a clay object stand upright. Children were not pushed into working at a much higher level due to the availability of technical assistance; instead, teachers learned to watch for the readiness of individual children and to help them move gradually through the various stages. Because the Technique Group incorporated both the Encouragement and the Observation/Discussion Group approaches, teacher training sessions were more complex and challenging. Teachers had to become familiar with the clay medium to be able to offer children meaningful suggestions about appropriate techniques.

In addition to the three teaching groups which used strategies, a Control Group was established to determine the effects of a regular prekindergarten or kindergarten program on cognitive and affective development. While clay of some type might be available to children in these Control Group classes, it was typically offered as a special material in an activity center rather than as a class activity. Rarely was clay used in a regularly scheduled manner, particularly the earth type clays. Some of the reasons for this ignoring of clay in the classroom have already been discussed. It is hoped that this book will help teachers find ways to put clay into classroom, especially after discovering what clay can do for children. The Control Group was in part established so that the question could be answered as to whether an unstructured approach to clay activity can assist children in developing cognitively and affectively.

Children of the Research

In both the United States Phase Two research and the Israeli study, children who became part of the research shared many characteristics. Despite differences between the two cultures, children in both countries shared the predicament of early academic failure, hindering future progress in school, and low verbal and language performance. Since the Israeli study was conducted first, many of the insights about the characteristics and the needs of children who need special assistance in order to be prepared to meet the challenges of today's schools were available to provide information for the American study. The addition of new testing materials, a larger sample, and revisions of Israeli procedures and tests meant that results of the two studies should not be compared directly on each finding. However, many factors are similar enough to provide information regarding how children in both cultures can be helped in their cognitive and affective learning through the use of clay in the classroom.

In Columbus, as in many other large metropolitan centers, there are sections of the city which are classified as poverty areas, where housing is often substandard and a high number of families receive some type of welfare assistance. Until court-ordered desegregation was instituted in the Columbus Public Schools in the late seventies, there were particular schools within the Columbus system which had high percentages of students whose families were receiving aid to dependent children (ADC) support. Those schools with the highest numbers of such children qualified for a number of ESEA Title I funds, and were designated as Priority I and Priority II schools. Other organizations in addition to schools attempted to deal with factors which impacted upon the educational system. Problems such as poverty, unemployment, lack of medical care, excessive mobility, and poor human relations were recognized as contributing directly to the disadvantaged child's lack of readiness for the schooling process.

Disadvantaged children in Columbus have historically come from families which are black or from a white Applachian background. Both groups originally came to Columbus from areas where potential upward movement in the standard of living seemed less possible. For some, there were opportunities to break away from the chain of previous failures and frustrations, but many blacks and whites found themselves living in urban ghetto-like conditions. Children from homes in these areas often found school to be a place where they could be certain of two meals and a warm, dry room. Teachers recognized that for many of these children, learning as defined by schools was a difficult process, one which required a kind of language many children had never encountered. Testing of children entering the Columbus schools indicated the lack of readiness of the disadvantaged child. Scores of first grade readiness revealed that of the children in the Priority I and II schools, 35.5% fell below expectancy levels. Compare this to the sample of non-priority school children, 9.5% of whom tested below expectancy level on the same test.

42

As the disadvantaged child moves through the early elementary years, the pattern of failure often accelerates. The pattern of failure in Columbus can be traced by comparison of scores on reading tests which show that not only does the proportion of children falling below expectancy level increase with the number of years spent in school, but the gap between achievement and expectancy widens as well.

Whereas the population of disadvantaged children in Columbus came primarily from black and Appalachian white backgrounds, in Tel Aviv the children from less advantaged background were from Middle Eastern and North African countries. Successive waves of immigration brought to Israel within a comparatively short time people from more than fifty countries. The Jewish immigrants from the Middle Eastern and North African countries brought with them influences of religious, agrarian, social, and cultural characteristics. Many of the Middle Eastern and North African people created patterns of living far different than those of the rest of the Israeli population, who were generally of Middle Eastern European origins. The existing social and economic patterns had been evolved by those immigrants who came from the more urbanized and industralized European countries. Many of the Middle Eastern and North African immigrants found it difficult to fit into the structure of life. For many immigrants, life was concentrated into urban neighborhoods, some of which became slums. The low vocational and educational levels, poorly paid and unstable employment, and a high birth rate started a vicious cycle for many families. Language difficulties added to the frustration, especially for the children who were expected to be prepared to read and speak Hebrew, the language used in Israeli schools.

Despite the considerable effort invested by the State of Israel to bridge the cultural and economic gaps, particularly in an extensive program for preschool aged children, reading skills and comprehension as well as arithmetic skills were considerably lower for those from the Middle Eastern and North African backgrounds. The gaps became even more apparent in second grade (Smilansky, 1976), adversely affecting both children and their families. School failure causes grave disturbances in family life. In the Israeli culture, education and success in school are promises of a better future for children, as well as a status symbol and means of social mobility for parents. In the eyes of some parents, a child's early failure in school undermines the parents' confidence in their capacity to help the child achieve an education.

For children in Columbus or Tel Aviv, failure in school causes problems which go beyond the classroom door. Success in school is important, particularly during the early years, when patterns are established for the remainder of the child's schooling. Children in nursery school and kindergarten need to develop abilities which can be essential to later success in school; this success is directly tied to eventual ability to become a productive member of society. For a great many young children, success can come at an early age when the arts are included as an important part of the curriculum.

During the Phase Two (second year) of the Columbus project, 27 schools with 39 teachers and their classrooms participated in the research study. Priority I and II schools were utilized; these were those with a high concentration (over 38%) of children whose families received aid for dependent children. Schools also had to have both prekindergarten and kindergarten classes which were not involved in other experiments. The interest of the principal and the teachers was an important criteria used in identifying schools for the clay project. In addition to the teachers participating in the three experimental groups, fourteen teachers and their classrooms were selected for the Control Group. A few schools were paired in order to provide both prekindergarten and kindergarten classes within the control group. Altogether, about 1600 children participated in the classroom experiment during Phase Two; of these, a random sample of 326 children were both pre and posttested. In comparison, the Israeli study included four groups of kindergarten children, with about 40 children in each group. Because of the structure of kindergarten classrooms in Israel, teachers worked with smaller groups of children than did the American teachers.

In Columbus, to test the central question of the research, four groups of children were randomly selected. Each group included four and five year olds in the selected schools. To control contamination between groups, such as discussions between teachers regarding particular strategies being used at a given school, the evaluation department of the Columbus schools clustered the identified schools into four groups which were geographically divided by school regions. To assure similar populations within all groups, the clusters of schools were arranged to include a similar range of percentages (between 38 and 81% for the entire cluster) of ADC children in each group.

About 10 or 12 children from each of the 53 classrooms were randomly selected to be tested before and after the 16 week intervention period. These tested children had to fall within certain age groupings: prekindergarten children between 48 and 68 months; kindergarten children between 68 and 72 months. The goal was to test an equal number of boys and girls, prekindergarten and kindergarten, in each intervention and control group. Although 510 child-

TABLE 1   NUMBER OF CHILDREN PRETESTED AND POSTTESTED IN EACH INTERVENTION GROUP, GRADE, SEX

GROUP	PREKINDERGARTEN			KINDERGARTEN			
	Boys	Girls	Total Pre-k.	Boys	Girls	Total Kdg.	Total Intervention Group
Encouragement	18	21	39	22	20	42	81
Observation/ Discussion	22	22	44	20	19	39	83
Technique	23	17	40	20	25	45	85
Control	19	20	39	18	20	38	77
Total by Grade and Sex	82	80	162	80	84	164	326

ren were pretested, only 326 were posttested; this was due to such factors as children moving or being excessively absent. There were 162 prekindergarten and 164 kindergarten children tested, and of these 162 were boys and 164 girls. Table 1 indicates how the groups were arranged in terms of numbers and groupings.

The Testing Process

In order to fully assess the results of any intervention or lack of intervention on children in the clay project, a series of pre and post-testing materials were devised. Some of these, such as the Clay Verbs Test, were first used in Israel and later refined in Phase One of the Columbus study. All instruments for testing were designed to be used by classroom teachers to assess children's levels of perform-ance and progress in the particular skills being studied: clay, drawing, and verbal. Those tests which were devised by the project staff in-cluded a scale for evaluating sculptural abilities of young children and the sculptural evaluation of clay products made by the clay project children. Tests for the assessment of verbal cognition were selected from available standardized tests in use in the United States.

Both before and after the 16 week intervention period, each child was asked to make a clay object during each of three testing sessions: a free choice, a dog, and a person. Testers were substitute teachers employed by the Columbus schools on a regular basis as substitutes in the elementary grades. Many hours of training were provided to insure that each teacher-tester understood the pro-cedures to be used in the pre and posttesting sessions. It was extreme-ly important that children felt comfortable with the teacher-testers; it was also vital that no tester bias enter into the results. The clay project staff also assisted with evaluations of the testers periodically; some testing of children was done by the staff as well. The clay pieces made during the testing periods were evaluated by the teacher-testers using the Cognitive Clay Scale and the Sculptural

46

Clay Scale. Both of these scales had been validated previous to the testing sessions.

Dogs were included in the 16 week intervention topics used by both the Observation/Discussion Group and the Technique Group teachers. Children were asked to make a dog in the pre and post-testing periods in order to see if changes in performance occurred from a taught subject. Specifically not included in the intervention topics, a clay person was part of the testing process in order to assess transfer from a taught to an untaught subject. The third category of clay objects was a free choice, so that children were offered the opportunity to create anything they wished with the clay during the pre and posttesting periods. This provided evaluators with the chance to observe what children would do with clay when they could choose their own subject matter.

The Cognitive Clay Scale was used by teachers to examine the clay products in terms of their recognizability; the number of physical details; how many details were correctly placed; the number of details which were three-dimensional; proportions; whether the product was one piece of clay or not; and what techniques were utilized in making the clay piece. All of these aspects relate to how individual children reveal knowledge and understanding about their worlds. Also examined in the scale was a child's ability to use the clay three-dimensionally as compared to trying to regard it as another medium for drawing (e.g., using the clay to outline a figure flat on a table rather than building the figure upright or in a solid, rounded fashion) (Photographs of children's clay work can be found in the Appendix).

The Sculptural Clay Scale was used to examine the overall artistic and sculptural score. The terms artistic and sculptural will be clarified in Chapter Four. This scale evaluated any treatment of the surface of the clay; the use of sculptural space; the unity of the piece; the expressive qualities; and the use of the clay itself as a medium. Rather than looking for those characteristics of the clay piece which indicated the child's intellectual level, the creative and expressive qualities were also investigated. While complete separation of the cognitive clay and the sculptural clay aspects is not possible, much can be learned from close examinations of each of

47

these aspects as a distinct but linked area. There may be times as children develop when the cognitve understanding is far ahead of the artistic, and vice versa; the ability to recognize these variables so overtly through the clay medium is one of its many benefits for the classroom teacher.

To study any transfer of change in performance from one medium to another, drawing was included as a task in the testing sessions. Each student was asked to draw a free choice subject, a dog, and a person. Testers mixed the tasks so that the same subject in clay as in drawing was not done during the same test session. The Harris-Goodenough Drawing Scale was used to evaluate the drawing of the person. Drawings of the dog and the free choice were evaluated on the basis of the Cognitive Drawing Observation Scale, closely based upon the Harris-Goodenough Scale. The drawing observation scale and the Cognitive Clay Scale were very similar, making comparisons possible. Both scales looked at recognizability; number of physical details, and their correct placement; proportions; and the technique used. Not included in the drawing scale were the three-dimensional and whole figure sections since these would not be appropriate to two-dimensional products. Perspective was included in the drawing scale, and was intended to determine a child's ability to represent three-dimensional concepts in a two-dimensional medium.

The assessment package also included a comprehensive set of instruments to measure verbal cognition, and comprised the major portions of the data collection instruments relative to student objectives. The Clay Verbs Test examined the comprehension and vocabulary development; the Test of Verbal Enumeration, also referred to as the Duplicates Test, compared a child's verbal description of a dog or person with that child's clay dog or person; and the Wechsler Preschool and Primary Scale of Intelligence (which included five subtests) provided a verbal IQ score. Table 2 provides a summary of the testing package components.

TABLE 2   TESTING INSTRUMENTS USED IN THE CLAY PROJECT
PRE AND POSTTESTING

Instrument	Area of Assessment
Sculptural Clay Scale	Clay sculpturing/artistic ability
Cognitive Clay Scale	Clay sculpturing/cognitive ability
Drawing Observation Scale	Drawing cognitive ability
Harris-Goodenough Draw-a-Man Test	Drawing cognitive ability and performance IQ
Clay Verbs Test	Comprehension and vocabulary development
Test of Verbal Enumeration (Duplicates)	Concept development, verbal fluency and organization
Wechsler Preschool and Primary Scale of Intelligence (WPPSI)	Verbal IQ

Due to the depth of the testing package, children were given the components during four separate sessions, usually spread out over a week. One teacher worked with one child at a time. Due to the variety of intervention strategies, the project staff tried to distribute the testers over several groups, and to vary the schools to which they were sent for pretest and posttest. The testing schedule was planned to minimize any systematic tester bias.

Classroom teachers were asked to assess children in their classes using the Teacher's Scale of Classroom Adjustment. This scale developed by Smilansky and Shephatia for studies done in Israel, assessed cognitive, social, and emotional adjustment of individual children in the classroom setting. The teacher rated each child on a one to five scale for each of 18 subtests, for each of six categories. Scores were totalled for a final adjustment score. The results were used in analyzing the relationship of children's classroom adjustment to their development in clay sculpturing.

To assist with the evaluation process of the clay products, photographs were taken of both the pre and post clay pieces. In addition, drawing were made by the testers of each clay product, with measurements and any descriptions based on the child's own talk about the work. Some photographs can be found throughout this book, as well as those taken of children during the clay activities in the classrooms. In many ways, the expressions seen on the children's faces provide vivid confirmation of otherwise dry and lifeless statistics!

Product vs. Process

Although more discussion of the importance of the process of working in clay to the young child will be discussed in Chapter Three, it seems appropriate to at least mention in the overview of how children's clay pieces were evaluated the product vs. process concerns. To the young child, it is the process of making an object out of the clay, or the pure enjoyment of manipulating the medium, which is of prime importance. In many respects, the result of the process, the product, is secondary. The clay project staff was fully aware of this phenomenon, which is also apparent in other art media as well. However, if the goal is to study the work of young children to discover clues about their growth and development in order to assist them, then collecting and evaluating art works of young children can be of vital importance. As teachers in the classrooms soon discovered, the four and five year olds had no problem with putting back the clay each day so it could be remoistened and be ready to use next time. In fact, the adults had more concerns about the clay pieces made by the children than did the children themselves! Elliot Eisner has pointed out that what children do as they create is a "Consequence of process, processes that are internally operant and nonempirical. What children produce whether in the formative stages of work or in its conclusion are products of those processes. We can have products only through process, and can 'know' processes only through products." (Eisner, 1972).

50

The processes contain the seeds of the way in which children make sense of their worlds. Careful examination of both the process and the result of that process can provide valuable information to teachers regarding the cognitive and affective skills of the young child. Only by understanding where the child is can he or she be helped by teachers to move to a higher level. Through clay in the classroom, teachers can gain this understanding at the same time the child is preparing to take those steps toward further development.

3

CLAY: TEACHING WITH IT

Preparing Teachers

Exposing a group of teachers to strategies for using clay in a classroom setting for the first time can have its amusing aspects! One such introduction to clay came just as the Phase Two year of the Columbus research was about to begin. Almost one hundred teachers and aides gathered in one large room for an all day workshop of training for participants in the clay project. For some teachers and aides, the thought of using clay with more than 20 children at once was asking for trouble. It was delightful to see that all but the most skeptical had changed their minds after spending a short amount of time experiencing and learning about clay. For the more skeptical, several additional sessions of clay activities being done in the classroom was required; eventually, those teachers who came to teach with the clay during the research realized that clay was in fact not in itself the messy, hard-to-control medium many thought it to be. Part of the secret turned out to be how the clay was managed: its preparation, distribution, storage, and cleanup. Each teacher found ways to fit clay into the ongoing life of the classroom, sometimes in quite ingenious ways. Chapter Six, Clay in Your Classroom, provides examples of clay management techniques and specific information about the how-tos and don'ts.

For the purpose of the clay project research, teaching with clay was much more intense and concentrated than in a typical classroom situation. During a 16 week period, teachers provided children with clay 32 times, each at least a half hour in length. The workshop mentioned in the first paragraph helped prepare teachers for the experience. Because teachers were not yet aware of which methodology they would be using, or even what the various strategies would be, the workshop was a general look at clay in the classroom and related materials. There were four goals regarding the overall training of teachers for the clay project:

1. to alleviate misgiving about the messiness of clay and management problems in the classroom.

54

2. to help in the understanding and acceptance of the theoretical reasons for using clay as a medium to develop language and cognition within the particular intervention method of each group.
3. to train teachers how to use the particular strategy assigned to them.
4. to teach assessment of a child's clay process and product and use it as a basis for intevention.

During the workshop, experiences in expressing concepts (a dog) in dramatic play, drawing, language, and clay were provided. By presenting a variety of media experiences, it was hoped that participants of the workshop could better understand the contributions and unique requirements of each media in cognitive, affective, and psychomotor areas. This understanding provided a basis for discussing the rationale of the clay project. To further emphasize the management aspects of clay, that part of the day's experience was conducted as it would have been in a normal classroom setting. Teachers and aides had the opportunity to interact with the clay from the child's point of view as well as observing others from the teacher's viewpoint.

Subsequent seminars were conducted separately for each intervention group; this was to avoid contamination of the method being studied. (Chapter Two describes how groups were selected and arranged). Each of the three staff members, Hagan, Huddle and Lewis, trained and supervised one of the three groups. During the training seminars, teachers were encouraged to feel that they were partners in the study, and that their suggestions were welcomed. The theory for each intervention method was clarified and teaching techniques were developed during these meetings. As much as possible, the clay objectives were related to the various objectives which prekindergarten and kindergarten teachers were expected to meet during the school year. Examples of some of these objectives were counting, naming shapes, and learning basic concepts such as over and under. With clay, children could experience these concepts rather than simply memorizing or naming. A four year old who had just made 23 balls of clay was delighted to count (with help the first time) the balls and report the results to the class. A class of five year olds put all their just-made clay objects together on a table in the room; they compared the pieces according to shape, size, height, length, etc. The amount of cognitive information packed into one clay period amazed many of the project teachers. Particularly in the Observation/Discussion Group and the Technique Group, bringing a range of expectations, both artistic and cognitive, to each lesson was not only possible, it was a vital part of the ongoing process.

Within each intervention group or teaching strategy, the interaction between teachers and children was crucial to the research study. Only by carefully monitoring the way which children responded to the different types of teaching techniques could accurate assessments be made concerning how children were able to strengthen skills in cognitive and affective areas. For this reason, Hagan, Huddle, and Lewis spent much of their time during the Phase Two year visiting classrooms, keeping written records of how both class and teacher were doing in regard to the particular intervention style being used, and assisting those teachers who needed additional information or advice. Several monitoring instruments were utilized by the project staff to help determine how the strategy was being implemented by individual teachers as well as changes in attitudes towards clay. During the four months of clay activities in various classrooms (times were staggered so that not all schools were involved in the clay sessions at once), there were additional meetings with all teachers within a particular teaching strategy. All Technique Group teachers at one school might meet together for an hour to talk over the next week's lesson; at another time, several schools in the same group might hold a work session to learn a new technique. Newsletters for each of the three methods helped keep ideas flowing, and provided ways for teachers to share in the efforts of others.

Sixteen Weeks of Clay

The Encouragement Group did not use topics during the 16 weeks of clay in the classroom. This was not part of their intervention strategy. However, both the Observation/Discussion Group and the Technique Group used set topics for all but three of the 16 weeks.

56

Earlier mention was made of the way in which the topics were chosen: the Israeli study, the Phase One results, and the appropriateness of the subject to the medium of clay were all considered in the decision as to which topics should be used. The order in which the topics were arranged was decided by the complexity of each and its relationship to other subjects. Particularly in the Technique Group, it was necessary to allow for a range of skills to be accommodated with each topic; in this way, those children ready to move to higher levels could do so.

The three weeks (nine sessions) of free choice clay activities provided valuable information both to teachers and to the project staff. The first free choice sessions, during the first week, allowed time for children unfamiliar with clay (almost all children since few had ever used earth clay) to explore and investigate without the expectation of a product. These two beginning periods provided sufficient time for many of the children to become familiar enough with the clay to try making specific objects during the following weeks. For the younger or less experienced child, time was sometimes required at the beginning of a clay lesson to further explore the clay before going on to a particular task. Other children seemed to need to return periodically to some of the beginning levels, usually moving through these as if to reinforce some understanding of the clay medium before moving on to more complex forms. The free choice session at the halfway point and at the last week were particularly interesting since it was at these points that children clearly indicated to teachers what concepts and skills they had integrated into their own thinking and understanding.

A look at the topics used during the 16 week period indicates the movement from simple to more complex subjects as well as how ideas were "stacked" over several weeks to provide continuity:

1. Free choice (introduction to clay)
2. Pottery: Making a bowl
3. Foods: What fits in a bowl?
4. Dog
5. Dog with food that fits in an bowl
6. Birds

7. Birds with nest
8. Free choice
9. Farm or domestic animals
10. Vehicles (could relate to farm)
11. Pottery: Making a vase
12. Zoo animals
13. Zoo animals with environment
14. Furniture
15. Houses with dog
16. Free choice

Children whose primary tools for expression have been paper, pencil, and crayons may at first attempt to use clay as a similar two-dimensional medium. Teachers found many children, particularly during the first weeks of working with clay, shaping flat, linear figures from the clay. These children tended to work close to the table surface and seemed unaware of those special characteristics of clay which allow it to be used three-dimensionally. Topics, particularly in the Columbus study, were deliberately chosen to help overcome the tendency to see clay as a two-dimensional medium. More rounded, sculptural forms such as bowls, birds, food, etc., seemed to in themselves encourage children to work three-dimensionally. A direct correlation had been found during Phase One between the subject and the degree of three-dimensionality of the product. This is important for teachers since it may be expecting too much of the young child with little experience to understand the unique characteristics of a particular medium without the assistance of the teacher, particularly in regard to the type of product expected.

The remainder of this chapter will be a look at each of the three methods, Encouragement, Observation/Discussion and Technique, and how each was utilized by teachers in the classroom setting. Although the research study looked at how children developed through clay activities used as part of the curriculum, teachers were a vital part of the study as well. Only through their efforts did the research take form, and through their enthusiasm did the children come to learn through the medium of clay. Chapter Four provides information about the findings which resulted from the three teaching strategies; Chapter Five presents brief personal glimpses of the children who were participants in the prekindergarten and kindergarten classrooms which used clay. These chapters together may assist those who are interested in how the theory behind the research was put into practice and the way in which clay in the classroom impacted upon both teachers and students.

Teaching with Encouragement

For most teachers, being supportive is a natural, even necessary expectation of themselves; it is part of their daily routine. Along with supportiveness, however, often comes a strong sense of the need to be directive in order for children to really learn. Children come to accept at early ages the authority figure called teacher and try to fulfill as many of the expectations of that person as possible. While this willingness to accept the teacher as the person who gives instructions and sets the standards is limited by the experience and the skills of the individual child (there may be some standards and instructions which the child cannot understand or which are beyond the child's capabilities), most young children believe that the teacher as a figure of authority is part of the schooling process.

Those teachers who were more directive in their instruction found that the nondirective expectations of the Encouragement Group part of the clay study were a challenge. Charlotte Huddle, the project staff person who trained the Encouragement Group teachers, spent many hours with teachers helping them discover ways to be encouraging without being commanding, to be supportive without being managerial, to be positive without being manipulative. Huddle pointed out during the sessions with teachers that almost all behavior of the young child, including that which is often called intellectual, is aimed at achieving a feeling of satisfaction. Feelings of self-worth, of confidence, of self-expression and of autonomy are important to a child. Teachers help create the climate in the classroom which allows individual children to find ways to develop such feelings. As much as intellectual and cognitive development may be stressed, especially in today's high technology world, little can occur regarding either the growth of intellect or cognition without the underlying emotional support needed.

As did the other two method groups, the Encouragement Group teachers had arranged times for children with clay twice a week for 16 weeks. Because no set topics were to be introduced, time could be spent in talking to individual children, and perhaps more importantly listening to children talk. Teachers spent a great deal of the clay period walking from one group of children to another, making appropriate comments ("You are making that clay go so high today!" "Show me how you made that texture on your clay; it is very nicely done . . ." "I can't wait to see what your clay piece will look like when it's finished!") A combination of labeling for the child what actions or steps have occurred as well as encouraging the looking and planning ahead to what might happen are important in the encouragement process. These ways of interacting with the children during clay sessions can develop vocabulary as well as support confidence and self-worth feelings. Teachers can gain valuable insight into how individual children process information and communicate ideas about their worlds.

To encourage children to express themselves both through the clay and verbally, teachers asked children to tell about what they were making with the clay. This story-telling aspect provided a means of discovery of what was going on inside a particular child's mind; about the interests, dislikes, fears, misconceptions, understandings, and enjoyments held by that child. What to an adult eye might look like lumps of unformed clay can hold rich amounts of material which the young child's imagination uses to communicate ideas. Encouragement Group teachers discovered that they needed to spend a little extra time with the exceptionally shy or least experienced children before ideas began to emerge. Time invested in encouraging these children to express themselves through the clay medium proved worthwhile both for what teachers were able to learn and how the child benefited affectively and cognitively.

Teachers in the Encouragement Group used the clay time occasionally to observe individual children for most of the period. Children engaged in clay activities offered to the observant teacher much

60

about style of learning, knowledge of particular subjects, socialization skill levels, tolerance for frustration, problem solving abilities, span of concentration, etc. Some teachers discovered that keeping a small notebook with a page for each child made it easy to jot down notes about a particular way in which children were interacting with the clay or with each other. As bits of information began to accumulate for some children, what seemed at first to be fragments began to form patterns and make sense. Teachers began to find ways to use some information gathered during clay periods for other activities during the day. One teacher in a prekindergarten class discovered a child during the clay time using a word frequently in such a way that it was clear the child did not understand the meaning of the word. Over a period of several days, the teacher made certain that the word was used in its correct sense while classroom activities continued. The child was thus allowed the satisfaction of using the word correctly during the next clay period, transferring the knowledge of what the word meant from one context to another — an important skill needed by children to succeed in the schooling process.

During the encouragement clay sessions, teachers were able to incorporate many of the objectives of the prekindergarten and kindergarten language arts curriculum guide. Four areas, discrimination, relating, sequencing, and classifying were part of the curriculum; in each of these areas, many skills could be built during the clay activities. Because the Encouragement Group teachers could not direct children to such concepts by specific lesson planning or suggesting that certain activities be done, they instead watched for children to do with the clay some of the particular areas and then encourage them by labeling what they were doing and reinforcing the behavior. The areas and some of the ways in which clay assists to develop each are as follows:

Discrimination

Make comparisons	Distinguish shape, size
Eye/hand coordination	Find what is missing
Isolate differences	Recognize rhythm

Relating

Understand beginning, middle, end

Understand first to last

Work from left to right

Seriate

Classify

Make inferences

Generalize patterns

Know body parts

Dramatize/roleplay

Sequence

Know top to bottom and vice
versa

Understand graduated sizes

Tell a story with a beginning, middle and end

For the teachers who learned to use the encouragement methods, the clay periods provided many and varied ways to be "with" children. There was a freedom from needing to judge whether something the child was making was right or wrong. Individual children could be accepted wherever they happened to be developmentally, and a better perception gained as to where they might be able to go in terms of both their affective and cognitive growth. Spending time with individual children as they worked with clay meant teachers could discover more about each child's individual interests and needs. From such a small amount of investment, both timewise and financially, came much to provide teachers with improved ways to teach.

Teaching with Observation and Discussion

Possibly of the three methods, the one which seemed comfortable to teachers from the beginning was the Observation/Discussion Group. The strategy for teachers in this method was to combine the encouragement approach with somewhat more direction and a definite structure. Many teachers of prekindergarten and kindergarten-aged children felt this strategy was similar to that used by them in most classroom activities. However, the clay part of the study meant that teachers did need training in how this particular medium would fit into the strategy of encouragement and direction. Helen Lewis, who was the staff person supervising those six schools which made up the Observation/Discussion section, spent many hours with teachers helping them prepare for the classroom clay activities. First, of course, the teachers had to become familiar and comfortable with the clay medium. Then ways to interact with children with encouragement, using many of the same strategies discussed in the Encouragement Group section, were clarified. In addition, teachers in this group were expected to guide children through a series of lessons arranged and selected to assist in the cognitive and affective development.

When children are provided with experiences related to a particular subject, encouraged to talk about that subject, asked to look again at that subject (perhaps in a new way), and then to interpret that subject in clay, children can begin to develop a variety of cognitive skills. The planned series of topics utilized in both the Observation/Discussion and Technique Groups involved children in both observing and talking about each subject before clay pieces were made. Although exposed to the same motivational materials and discussions, children were not expected to make identical products; instead, support for individual exploration of each topic was provided. Time was planned so that children had time during the 16 weeks of the clay project to do experimentation, and to explore in their own ways subjects of their own chosing.

The Observation/Discussion Group teachers looked for ways to interest children in the various subjects. When children were able to identify with a topic, when it was made part of their own experiences, children could be expected to have the mental image of a concept which is required before that concept can be made with clay. Helping children of four and five years of age to "own" concepts was a concern of those teachers working with Lewis in the implementation of the Observation/Discussion strategy. To illustrate how the planning resulted in ways to introduce certain topics, the second week's subject, bowls, can serve as one example. During planning sessions, the teachers decided that bringing bowls to class to illustrate the varied sizes and shapes and sizes would make a good introduction. Children were allowed to handle, observe and discuss the bowls. During discussions, teachers asked children to explain how bowls were used at their homes and how a favorite bowl looked. The story of *Goldilocks and the Three Bears* was read in many classrooms to illustrate the use of bowls. Lively talks about the three sizes of bowls and how much each could hold resulted. Snack time in classrooms often used a bowl, and the children were asked to explain why bowls needed sides and what made the inside and the outside of the bowl form (positive and negative space).

All of the activities preliminary to actually making the clay bowls allowed the children time to assimilate the concept of bowl, and to have that concept firmly in mind before forming a bowl shape. The child's own experiences created the sense of "bowlness" needed. In coming to understand that within the broader classification of bowls are many kinds and shapes, children were operating on a higher cognitive level than if they had accepted one bowl as being like all others. Skills such as generalization, differentiation, discrimination, and others, were called into operation through the bowl lessons. The third week, which had as its topic food in bowls, had already been introduced during the discussions about bowls to a large extent. Opportunities to make children aware of particular foods which need bowls and why, and what sizes of bowls are needed for certain foods, were discussed before the children made food and bowls. Again, higher levels of cognitive thinking were encouraged by the way in which the subject was presented.

Perceptual, cognitive, and verbal skills represented in clay experiences are not discrete and separable in their operation. They cannot be isolated for teaching; each interacts and depends on the other. In the clay lessons, however, teachers focused more on one skill area than another at certain times. Perhaps, for example, touching a variety of objects might be an excellent way of introducing a subject; another time, children might talk about how they felt about a certain experience they had which relates to a topic being discussed. Verbalizing (labeling, categorizing, describing) can expand the thinking process, forming a conceptual base for moving from the concrete to the abstract (forming a mental picture) and then back to the concrete again (making a clay piece). Unlike the teachers in the Encouragement Group, teachers in the Observation/Discussion Group did not wait for the child to do something with the clay before beginning an interaction about what the child was doing. Teachers stimulated and challenged children to make something with the clay.

64

This stimulation and challenge was based upon the preparation children had received: looking, talking, touching, and each of these activities related to a concept related to the world of the individual child.

In both the Encouragement and Observation/Discussion Groups. the teachers were not to give children information or suggestions about the technical aspects of making objects from clay. If a child was struggling to make a clay piece stand upright, the teacher could encourage that child to look for ways to solve the problem (What is it that makes the dog stand? How many legs does he have? Should we go and see?) Children were expected to do their own problem-solving with the support and encouragement of the teacher. Children were reminded, when a clay piece crumbled beyond the point of repairability, that clay was easy to shape back into a ball and that another try might result in an even better clay piece that before. The forming qualities of the clay medium allowed ideas to be shaped and reshaped, and children were encouraged to take advantage of this aspect of the clay. Teachers learned to wait until they heard an explanation about clay pieces before coming to a conclusion about how well a child might understand a subject. For example, a dog having two instead of four legs might mean that two of the legs "are underneath 'cause he's sitting down!" What might at first seem like a technical problem or a lack of understanding could, in fact, be perfectly valid once the child is given the chance to explain. And in providing time for individual children to talk about clay pieces, one of the goals of the project, to increase verbalization skills, was enhanced.

As in the Encouragement Group, teachers in the Observation/Discussion Group found that keeping record of individual children in a checklist or log fashion allowed patterns of problem solving behavior, socialization, information processing, and other behaviors to be noted in regard to any changes or needs. Teachers discovered individual children who had special qualities, and often could build on these qualities in other situations. Clustering of children with particular needs or at certain levels became less a matter of guessing and more determined by actual evidence. Thus, a group of five children who had shown a lack of awareness of what animals might live on a farm could be grouped together to look at books about farms, to talk about what animals do on a farm, and to play with a toy farm. The looking, touching, discussing method was utilized on all levels and with a range of skills to be developed depending on the level of the children involved.

Teaching with Technique

Because of the accumulative effect of the three methods, the third strategy for teaching with clay in the classroom required the most preparation of its teachers. Not only did the Technique Group teachers use encouragement and observation/discussion methods with children, they also helped children discover the unique characteristics of the clay medium itself. Teachers were expected to assist children regarding the technical aspects of the making of objects from clay. ("Why did the dog's legs all fall off? Well, let's see if we can find out why and do something about it!") Young children just beginning to discover the various ways in which clay responds to fingers and hands are not ready for indepth technical discussions and expectations concerning clay modeling. However, as individual children move from the basic levels of working in clay to the more advanced, there are simple but important technical aspects of making objects from clay which even young children can understand and from which they can benefit. ("Let me show you how I connected the leg on this dog I was making earlier. See how I smoothed the top of the leg into the body? Do you think you could try this and see if it would help make the legs stay on your dog, too?")

Having to know enough about clay to provide explanations about technical aspects was a challenge to teachers with little or no experience themselves in making objects with clay. Under the supervision of Judith Hagan, the art teacher on the project staff, the teachers spent many hours becoming acquainted with the medium of clay. In order to effectively present any one of the lessons, teachers had to be comfortable not only with ways in which to present the topic. but also with the strategies for how that particular topic could be created with the clay. An example is the pinchpot. One of the earliest techniques developed for creating simple bowl shapes, it is still a new idea to young children. Technique Group teachers had to first learn themselves how to create a variety of shapes with the pinchpot method, then they broke down the steps and tried to make them as clear and nonthreatening as possible for children of four and five years of age. Similar approaches were used for each topic, and teachers discovered that they did have the ability to learn what was required, and that this knowledge could be effectively presented to their classes.

As in the Observation/Discussion Method, it was vital that the teacher know the level of individual children so that each child could be best assisted in working with the clay. If a particular child was in the pounding stage, there was little point in trying to entice that child into making a pinchpot. However, ways to interest that child in rolling shapes with the clay, or cutting shapes from the clay after it was pounded, might provide incentive to move ahead into the next level of clay development. Usually, when given sufficient time to work with the clay, children moved rapidly through the earlier stages (see Chapter Six) of pounding, flattening, rolling, and drawing with the clay. While some children seemed to need to move back and forth between the more basic and somewhat advanced levels, as long as time to do this range of activities was provided on a regular basis, most children continued to move forward on a steady continuum. Teachers had to be knowledgable about the various ways in which children indicated readiness in working with the clay in order to assist them to move forward through the various clay stages. Only by offering support, both in terms of the emotional aspects and the needed cognitive skills, could teachers then expect children to be prepared to develop technical abilities as well.

Demonstration was an important part of the Technique Group Method. When children were expected to shape a pinchpot, they better understood the process after looking at examples of pots or bowls, including both "real" and photographed types. Discussing the various kinds of bowls children had in their homes helped establish a sense of identification with what bowls are for and their importance. As in the Observation/Discussion Group, teachers tried to find books and stories to read to their classes to further enhance the bowl image. Once it was clear that children understood the concept of bowl or pot, it was up to the teacher to create in the children a sense of the "magic" as they watched a bowl appear out of a ball of clay! Discovering clay should be an ongoing process for young children, and teachers can provide supportive but challenging environments in which the discovery process can occur. Using demonstration methods did not mean, however, that teachers only showed a particular technique once to the whole class. Instead, many teachers discovered that by carrying a ball of clay with them as they walked about the room as children worked, they could quickly show one or two or a table of children an idea; this also avoided the temptation to work directly with a child's clay piece, which can create many more problems than it might solve!

Clay activities must be regarded by children as enjoyable as well as opportunities for learning if they are to fully benefit from an ongoing program. If teachers spend too much time in explanation or discussion, children soon lose interest and eventually may decide that creating with clay is frustrating or boring. Short, encouraging, and informational demonstrations and explanations should be sprinkled throughout a clay time rather than being presented in large chunks or all at once. Teachers need to be aware of how much time is spent in experiencing compared to listening or observing. Experiencing includes both the activities used to prepare children for the clay lessons as well as working with the clay itself. The lesson about birds is one which indicates this multi-faceted approach to creating with clay. Children were prepared for the lesson by reading stories about birds, taking walks to look for birds, looking at pictures of birds, and talking about birds. In some classes, children sang about birds (or sang like birds!) and even roleplayed birds. All of these activities occurred over a period of several days, and some were repeated. Just previous to the making of birds with clay, the teacher did a brief demonstration showing one of several methods children might use to create their birds. (Chapter Six provides specific information on these methods). Children then got their clay and proceeded to try out their individual ideas about birds. Since lessons are repeated, opportunities to try several approaches were provided, as well as time to learn from mistakes and gain experience.

One of the advantages to children of having the more technical aspects of clay included in the teaching strategy, is that less time is required by children in the trial and error process of discovering what makes clay the medium that it is. Instead of giving up in frustration when the dog's legs simply will not stay on, even after repeated efforts to make them "stick," a child can remember what the teacher said might work or watch as the teacher (or the child across the table who picked up the idea earlier) demonstrates a possible solution. Children have more time in which to consider the concept to be created through the clay medium. Having the clay more under control allows children the satisfaction of feeling as though they can carry an idea through to its conclusion, with the clay responding as expected — or when, for some reason, the clay does do something unexpected, knowing what to do about the situation, whether it is correcting it or capitalizing on it ("The clay was too wet to let my dog stand up, so I made her lying in a bed with six puppies!")

Teachers in the Technique Group discovered that as their experience with helping children create with clay increased, so did their awareness of how to balance the various aspects of the technique strategies. As was pointed out in the Observation/Discussion Group description, the perceptual, cognitive and verbal skills represented in clay experiences are interdependent and cannot really be isolated in any one lesson. Added to this list of skills, in the strategy used in the Technique Group were the technical skills of working with clay. Teachers learned that emphasizing one area more than another at certain times and with certain topics was desirable, and often allowed children more opportunities to extend their skills. Thus, for example, using one of the two times children were to make zoo animals to emphasize shape and form, then the next for more discussion and work with the various details of certain animals allowed the various skills to grow more slowly and become more a part of each child's understanding. Also important in the technique sessions were the free choice times provided. At these times, teachers could begin to see clearly which children had actually utilized the intervention and were able to make use of various skills to create their own ideas as well as those assigned by the teacher. Those lessons in which children chose their own topics provided time for children to reevaluate what they had discovered about clay, and without any pressure to learn new skills or ideas, to "fool around" with the clay in spontaneous ways. What was clear, however, about the products made during these free times was that they owed a great deal to the skillbuilding which had preceded them. Without the structure of the specific lessons, it was doubtful that the level of skill shown both in the clay pieces themselves and in the kind of discussion about the pieces would have been as high.

Keeping track of individual children's progress by means of logs or other records proved extremely helpful to those teachers who tried to do so. The variety of ways in which individual students solved problems, either with the clay or with each other; socialized around the clay tables; processed the information provided, both regarding lesson content and specific technical skills as well; proved to be diverse and often helpful in understanding a child's behaviors in other contexts than the clay activities. The Technique Group teachers were helped to understand the various levels of clay skills present in each class, and how to work with small groups of children clustered together because they shared certain needs. Lessons were carefully prepared, just as they would be for a reading activity, to allow for several levels of skill.

Teaching with Clay: Alternating Strategies

Now that the three methods used in the clay research have been delineated, it is important to reemphasize that using clay in a regular program for children in the classroom would probably be spread out over the length of the school year and would involve more opportunities for teachers to utilize all three strategies, sometimes together, sometimes separately. Because each teacher has his or her own interests, goals and skills, no two teachers would ever approach teaching with clay in the classroom the same way. What is important, of course, is the intent: why is it important to provide children the opportunity to work with clay on an ongoing basis? As the research findings explained in the next chapter indicate, children who work with clay in a structured program do develop cognitively and affectively. If those children who work with clay happen to be of preschool age, they are being better prepared to meet the challenges of the coming schooling process.

It is not, therefore, as important that a teacher possess a high level of skill in producing clay objects; instead, what is vital is that the teacher have the understanding that clay is one medium of many which can make a difference in how children do in school. Once that awareness is held, the rest will follow. Yes, it is exciting to know about computers and software; to have the latest in educational games; to persuade the PTA to buy the best playground equipment. But don't ignore those media which have potential for giving children the ability to think, to conceptualize, to perceive, and to create; without these, there might be little that children will have to bring to all the hardware and equipment a school could buy. The familiar story of the small child who spends hours playing with the boxes in which the expensive toys were packed has many parallels for educators when it comes to providing children with what they really enjoy and need.

Strategies involving teaching with clay in the classroom setting directly parallel those used to teach many other areas as well. Giving a pat on the back on one occasion might mean more to a particular child than a hundred words; another time, a chance to talk about a certain subject could open up some new possibilities which otherwise would be unknown and untried. For the teacher with the determination to make clay become an important medium for learning, ways to make use of the characteristics of clay as part of the teaching process will begin to emerge almost without effort once the commitment has been made.

4

CLAY: LEARNING FROM IT

How to Use this Chapter

Earlier chapters have suggested the range and complexity of the research study upon which much of this book is based. For those unfamiliar with how research studies are organized, particularly studies with an empirical structure, reading the specifics of the Clay Project research results may be similar to reading a foreign language. Even for experienced researchers, the amount of data generated by the project can be almost overwhelming. Many studies, especially those from the social sciences areas, might involve a small sample of perhaps 25 to 50 subjects and may utilize one particular setting. The Clay Project included hundreds of children in over 50 classrooms from two countries, Israel and the United States. The pre and posttesting package used to evaluate a random sample from a large number of children enabled staff members to examine a number of variables. Because three teaching strategies or methods were used in addition to a control group, variables could be seen in relation to the individual strategies, or in regard to all experimental groups together as compared to the control group. Instead of a study with a narrow range of what was actually tested and evaluated, the Clay Project used a large population, an extensive testing process, and a long-term implementation of three teaching methods.

The intent of this chapter is not to overwhelm readers with pages of statistics and findings. Instead, selected from the large amount of available data are those findings which seem particularly appropriate for classroom teachers. Enough information will be provided to offer the necessary support for the findings. Those interested in the detailed statistical analyses may refer to the formal report of the Clay Project which is available from the Educational Resource Information Clearinghouse (ERIC) for Early Childhood Education

In Chapter Two, the six major questions asked by the Clay Project were given. Because findings based upon these questions form the basis of this chapter, repeating them might be helpful:

1. What is cognitive about clay sculpture?
2. What is artistic about clay sculpture?

3. Does teacher intervention in children's sculpture activities foster cognitive as well as artistic development?
4. Do children transfer what they have learned in clay activities to other artistic and cognitive tasks?
5. Does the strategy used in teaching clay activities make a difference in the development of children?
6. Which type of teaching strategy is best for which type of child according to age, sex, intelligence, social and emotional adjustment, and clay abilities of the child?

In the four major sections of this chapter, findings from the various tests (see Chapter Two) which were utilized by teachers to answer these questions will be organized as follows:

1. The influence of clay activities on children's sculptural and cognitive growth.
2. The influence of clay activities on children's verbal development.
3. The influence of clay activities on children's I.Q.
4. The influence of clay activities on children's drawing.

Each section will include information about the effect of the three teaching strategies and the Control Group, and differences, if any, due to age and gender. The chapter will conclude with a summary to help clarify ways in which classroom teachers might utilize findings to assist individual children to develop both cognitively and artistically.

1. The Influence of Clay Activities on Children's Sculptural and Cognitive Growth

Defining Sculptural and Cognitive

For purposes of the Clay Project, the terms sculptural and cognitive have been used as they relate to certain characteristics and aspects of young children's clay activities and products resulting from those activities. The establishment of ways to measure each of these characteristics was vital to the findings to be discussed. Chapter Two describes the tests used to study both the cognitive and sculptural areas. The degree of reliability and validity of the instruments used indicated that they were accurately able to provide teachers with the necessary means to do such evaluations. In other words, it was possible to isolate certain aspects of both cognitive and sculptural domains, and then to look at whether or not a particular teaching strategy had impact enough to create change, either cognitive or sculptural or both, in individual children.

Because of the medium used in the various teaching programs, the specific aspects examined by the scales, both cognitive and sculptural, had to be appropriate for a three-dimensional medium. For this reason the word sculptural, as it refers to the analysis of clay pieces made by children, is perhaps more appropriate than the word artistic. Whereas a person might be considered artistic in a variety of media (clay, paint, textiles), someone with sculptural abilities would be specifically skilled in three-dimensional media such as clay, wood, plaster, stone, etc. In discussing the work made by young children in clay, both terms can be applied, although the sculptural designation is more directly linked to the process of producing work in clay. The clay scale which was devised to assess the cognitive aspects of making objects in clay has been labeled the Cognitive Clay Scale; the other scale, which examined the more artistic aspects, has been called the Sculptural Clay Scale.

It is important to keep in mind that the purpose of isolating specific cognitive and artistic/sculptural aspects of young children's artwork lies in what the findings can tell teachers so that they might be better able to assist children in the learning process. Developing tests that are able to "get at" the various artistic and cognitive characteristics cannot be regarded as an end in itself. Instead, these types of measurement should be regarded as part of a larger picture, some elements of which cannot be isolated or even measured. Only when used in conjunction with the improvement of teaching and learning do the various components of the Clay Project testing package have importance and meaning.

Using the Cognitive Clay Scale, teachers looked at what children made in clay before and after the 16 week period of time during which children in the three intervention groups used clay at least twice a week. The scale looked at the following aspects:

Recognizability
Physical Details
Correctly Placed Details
Three-dimensional Details
Proportion
Whole Figure
Technique

A copy of the Cognitive Clay Scale can be found in the Appendix.

When all three teaching strategies, Encouragement, Discussion, and Technique (see Chapter Two for descriptions), are grouped together into what can be called an experimental cluster, this cluster can be compared to the group of children who formed the Control Group, or those in classrooms where clay was not provided as part of an ongoing program during the 16 week period. Looking at the products made during the pre and posttesting times (a dog, a person, and a free choice), and using the Cognitive Clay Scale to analyze these products, teachers found that children in the combined groups improved significantly in five of the seven subtests when compared to the Control Group. While the experimental cluster children made progress in all seven subtests, those which showed the most growth (Recognizability, Correctly Placed Details, Proportion, Whole Figure and Technique) are areas which indicate children were able to gain in their abilities to integrate and express through clay their perceptions of their world. Children in the experimental groups were also able to increase the concepts necessary to make sense of the information being presented and then processed in the classroom setting.

As might be expected, experimental cluster children improved most in the subject which was taught during the 16 week intervention, dog. However, significant gains were also made in the untaught subject, person, and in the subject of their own choice. Therefore, helping children in one subject area also improved a generalized clay ability which could then be used in expressing other subjects in clay.

Children in the Clay Project were either in prekindergarten or kindergarten; both grades in the experimental cluster improved more than the two grades in the Control Group in Recognizability, Physical Details, and Proportions. Within the experimental groups, kindergarten children made greater gains in integrative clay skills such as Correctly Placed Details and Proportions. Younger children improved in their level of differentiation, while the older children were more ready to utilize the experiences to develop skills of integration when working with clay. The Technique Group, which offered children encouragement, a range of observation and discussion experiences related to topics, and assistance in finding ways to deal with the medium of clay itself, was the group which helped both prekindergarten and kindergarten children to reach the highest levels of growth. Kindergarten children especially seemed able to gain cognitively in any group; even Control Group kindergarten children made significant gains in making more three-dimensional details and improving their techniques. Encouragement kindergarten children gained in four of seven subtests; Discussion kindergarten children in five of seven. In the Technique Group, both kindergarten and prekindergarten children gained in all seven subtests of the Cognitive Clay Scale. The teaching strategy which utilized the fullest range of methods to help children learn using the medium of clay was able to help both age groups make the most progress.

Looking at whether the pattern is any different when boys are compared to girls, the test results showed that the experimental cluster boys and girls gained very similarly. What is of particular interest, however, is that the boys in the Control Group made significant gains when compared to the girls in that group. This was true in all subtests except Whole Figure. Girls in the Control Group made no significant gains in clay cognitively. Therefore, while being in one of the experimental groups helped boys improve more, those boys in the Control Group improved their cognitive clay skills even without intervention! Clay is a medium which is natural for helping boys achieve cognitive growth.

78

| | TABLE 3 | MEANS, STANDARD DEVIATIONS, AND t-TESTS: ACHIEVEMENT OF CHILDREN IN EACH TEACHING PROGRAM ON THE COGNITIVE CLAY SCALE |

Cognitive Clay Scale	Pretest		Posttest		Mean Gain	Sig. of Gain
	Mean	S.D.	Mean	S.D.		
Person + Dog	ENCOURAGEMENT GROUP (N = 81)					
Recogn.	6.57	3.35	8.11	3.32	1.54	.05
Physical Det.	8.94	4.82	12.01	4.30	3.07	.001
Correctly Pl.	3.28	3.42	4.86	3.34	1.58	.01
Proportions	5.51	2.71	7.73	3.15	2.22	.001
3−D	3.44	3.08	4.04	3.79	.59	*
Whole Figure	9.40	2.63	9.24	2.29	- .16	*
Technique	7.30	2.92	8.35	3.13	1.09	.05
	DISCUSSION GROUP (N = 83)					
Recogn.	6.06	3.56	8.77	4.06	2.71	.001
Physical Det.	9.06	5.34	11.46	5.59	2.40	.052
Correctly Pl.	4.12	3.45	4.69	4.01	.57	*
Proportions	5.33	3.31	7.25	3.72	1.93	.001
3−D	3.67	3.17	6.96	4.69	3.27	.001
Whole Figure	9.36	2.43	10.22	2.42	.86	*
Technique	6.10	3.57	8.95	4.10	2.80	.001
	TECHNIQUE GROUP (N = 85)					
Recogn.	6.27	3.94	10.60	4.35	4.33	.001
Physical Det.	8.13	5.42	14.13	6.41	6.00	.001
Correctly Pl.	2.88	3.37	7.38	4.56	4.51	.001
Proportions	4.84	3.22	8.88	4.32	4.05	.001
3−D	4.38	4.21	7.35	3.89	2.94	.001
Whole Figure	8.98	2.90	10.81	2.07	1.84	.001
Technique	6.94	2.86	10.61	4.32	3.73	.001

TABLE 3 (cont.)

	CONTROL GROUP (N = 77)					
Recogn.	6.30	3.75	7.07	3.85	.77	*
Physical Det.	8.75	5.10	10.20	5.04	1.46	*
Correctly Pl.	3.14	3.45	4.24	3.66	1.05	*
Proportions	5.20	3.10	6.24	3.57	1.04	.05
3−D	2.85	3.18	4.32	4.10	1.49	.05
Whole Figure	9.23	2.70	9.07	2.12	−.17	*
Technique	5.60	3.08	7.16	3.50	1.56	.05

* No Significant Gain

What do the findings from this scale tell teachers about teaching strategies? Table 3 indicates that it is the Technique Group which offers the most opportunities for teachers to assist children in their cognitive growth.

In each subtest, it is the Technique Group which significantly was able to improve cognitive skills. Recognizability, for example, showed improvement in all three experimental groups. In this subtest, children's clay pieces (dog or person) were compared to a series of photographs of clay products which ranged from lumps to recognizable figures. When children had to figure out their own way to express concepts, progress was slower. The child who had regular experiences with clay in an encouraging atmosphere also made gains in Recognizability, but less than other groups. Teachers in the Encouragement Group expected children to deal with the medium on their own, including discovering their own subjects and needs for observation. Each child therefore drew on his or her own experiences rather than those which a teacher might have introduced as part of the structure of a clay lesson. Both cognitive and psychomotor skills had to be gained through exploration, trial and error, and depended on reinforcement from the teacher and each child's own sensory feedback. Over 16 weeks (32 sessions) of clay lessons, children made progess in Recognizability in direct relationship to the amount of help the teaching program included: the number of aspects of potential growth in which a teacher could intervene, and did.

A similar pattern can be seen in the other subtests. In Physical Details, the children in the Technique Group went from a pretest mean of eight details to 14.1 details on the posttest. Children were able to learn how to observe and how to represent detail because of the technical training received during the 16 weeks. Even in the Encouragement Group, just working with clay and representing what they knew best did increase awareness and discrimination skills. Their gains were higher than those of children in the Discussion Group, who began intervention with more details than the other groups. In Whole Figure, which is the ability to make a figure whole and upright, the Technique Group was the only one to show gains. This indicates that to make a figure stand up requires knowing some techniques for getting the clay to "work." Another contributing factor was as children learned details and proportions, they concentrated on these and not on making the figure upright. Upright persons were harder to achieve than upright dogs; even the Technique Group children did not make gains in making standing people!

Even if a dog or person made of clay is lying down, it can have parts which are three-dimensionally interpreted. Children in both the Technique and Discussion Groups made significant growth in this subtest, Three-dimensional Details. Increased observation even in the Discussion Group, where no clay techniques were taught, increased children's awareness of multiple dimensions of their environment which they, in turn, could represent in clay. Proportions, which looked at the relationship of parts of the figure to the whole, showed growth in all groups, including the Control Group. Therefore, proportion skills seem to develop more as a result of maturation, but clay activities can accelerate that development. In the results from the subtest Technique, which evaluated the ability to utilize clay as a medium, all groups again showed gains, although, not surprisingly, Technique Group children were able to indicate the most growth in this area.

To summarize, teachers who offered children opportunities for clay activity in a supportive atmosphere and assisted in the children's understanding of themselves and sensory feedback, were able to assist children in improving their cognitive clay capabilities. When teachers gave children cognitive stimulation through guided experiences in a supportive atmosphere, intervening in the ordering of self, concept, sensory feedback and percept, children improved even more in their ability to learn through clay. "Knowing" the subject more helped them express more. When teachers gave children cognitive stimulation through guided experiences in a supportive atmosphere and helped them know how to make the clay respond to their ideas, intervening in their ordering of concepts, self, hand, clay, shapes, sensory feedback and percepts, children were able to improve the most in their cognitive capabilities as shown through the medium of clay.

Clay Activities and Sculptural Growth

Teachers analyzed the sculptural or artistic aspects of children's pre and posttest work in clay using the Sculptural Clay Scale. The dog, person and free choice clay sculptures were evaluated according to the following:

Surface Treatment
Sculptural Space
Unity
Expression
Utility

A copy of the Sculptural Clay Scale can be found in the Appendix. In addition to the five subtests, an Overall rating was given before the sculpture piece was evaluated from a more divided perspective.

Findings from the scale indicate that after 16 weeks (32 sessions) of clay activities in the classroom, the experimental cluster improved significantly in all subtests except Surface Treatment. Teachers using one of the three teaching strategies were able to assist children to become better from a sculptural as well as cognitive point of view. Children in the experimental cluster grew in their ability to express a concept, in the use of detail, in their ability to relate those details to the total or whole concept being expressed, and at the same time the aesthetic qualities of the expression were improved.

In looking at the differences between prekindergarten and kindergarten children, those in the experimental cluster improved significantly more than the Control Group children at both grade levels. Differences in gains were smaller between the kindergarten experimental children and those in the Control Group. Kindergarten children, because they were older, were able to make more progress than the prekindergarten Control Group children. While intervention methods with the clay activities benefited both younger and older children sculpturally as well as cognitively, the younger children made improvement sculpturally *only* when they had intervention. In fact, prekindergarten children who were in one of the three experimental groups made scores similar to the Control Group kindergarten children who were a year older.

Differences between boys and girls within the three experimental groups were negligible. However, differences between the experimental cluster girls and the Control Group girls were greater than those between the experimental cluster boys and the boys in the Control Group. While intervention methods helped both boys and girls to grow in sculptural clay achievement, girls made almost no improvement without intervention. Again, as was seen in the findings from the Cognitive Clay Scale, clay would seem to be a natural mode of expression for boys, not only cognitively but sculpturally as well.

One of the primary concerns of teachers involved in the Clay Project was to investigate whether or not intervening in activities involving an artistic medium would stifle or destroy a child's expression and creativity. Would the most directive teaching strategy, Technique, have a negative effect on the sculptural or artistic achievement of the child even if he or she were helped to develop cognitively?

A look at Table 4 will indicate that, similarly to the results found in the Cognitive Clay Scale, the more intervention provided, the more growth was made by children regarding their sculptural clay skills.

TABLE 4   MEANS, STANDARD DEVIATIONS, AND t-TESTS: ACHIEVEMENT OF CHILDREN IN EACH TEACHING PROGRAM ON THE SCULPTURAL CLAY SCALE

Sculptural Clay		Pretest		Posttest		Mean Gain	Sig. of. Gain
		Mean	S.D.	Mean	S.D.		
Person + Dog	N	ENCOURAGEMENT					
Overall	80	5.03	1.58	5.70	1.31	.67	.051
Surface	56	4.44	1.25	4.70	1.12	.26	*
Space	56	5.44	1.52	5.61	1.65	.17	*
Unity	56	5.60	1.72	6.26	1.60	.66	.05
Expression	56	5.40	2.25	6.51	1.64	1.11	.01
Utility	56	5.21	1.85	6.04	1.70	.83	.01
Average	56	5.18	1.70	5.86	1.37	.68	.01
		DISCUSSION					
Overall	77	5.09	1.72	6.58	1.74	1.49	.01
Surface	53	4.45	1.16	4.57	.98	.12	*
Space	53	5.32	1.47	6.98	2.11	1.60	.01
Unity	53	5.38	1.62	7.22	1.92	1.89	.01
Expression	53	5.52	2.00	7.26	2.59	1.79	.01
Utility	53	5.54	1.63	7.32	1.98	1.78	.01
Average	53	5.25	1.42	6.85	1.63	1.60	.01

TABLE 4 (cont.)

		TECHNIQUE					
Overall	70	5.03	1.89	8.46	2.48	3.43	.001
Surface	47	4.27	1.24	6.18	1.98	1.91	.01
Space	47	5.33	1.83	8.62	2.84	3.29	.001
Unity	47	5.27	1.80	7.41	2.72	2.17	.001
Expression	47	6.00	2.81	9.56	3.01	3.56	.001
Utility	47	5.22	1.98	9.09	2.89	3.87	.001
Average	47	5.18	1.93	8.60	2.40	3.42	.001
		CONTROL					
Overall	77	5.14	1.81	5.65	1.88	.51	*
Surface	51	4.47	1.15	4.79	1.33	.32	*
Space	51	5.18	1.79	5.42	2.00	.24	*
Unity	51	5.27	1.91	5.90	2.39	.63	*
Expression	51	5.55	2.23	6.50	2.65	.95	*
Utility	51	5.00	1.77	5.73	2.22	.73	*
Average	51	5.04	1.79	5.69	2.01	.65	*

* No Significant Gain

Children in the Control Group made no significant gains in any subtest of the Sculptural Clay Scale. Only with technical instruction did children improve in their ability to treat the surface of their clay pieces (adding textures, patterns, etc.) Results from the Encouragement Group showed that if children are given opportunities to work with clay, they will improve in their sculptural abilities particularly in regard to Unity, Expression and Utility. Any intervention and continued opportunity to use clay in a supportive atmosphere helped

85

children develop their sculptural capabilities. Intervention methods which included experiences with subject matter, teaching of techniques of working with clay, and continued opportunities to use clay in a supportive classroom setting, enhanced rather than retarded children's artistic expression and growth in clay.

Technique Group children, who received the most direction, including methods of working with the clay as a medium, were able to show progress in all subtests of the Sculptural Clay Scale. Contrasted with this growth is that of the Control Group, where children made no gains in any subtest.

In summary, it is possible to conclude that the two teaching strategies which focused directly on cognitive aspects of clay sculpturing, Technique and Discussion, were also the two strategies which were able to help children grow the most in relation to their artistic, or sculptural, abilities. With guidance in observation and discussion plus assistance in dealing with the clay medium, children were able to improve both cognitively and artistically. Children who did not have such guidance did not make artistic improvement on their own.

II. The Influence of Clay Activities on Children's Verbal Development

Anyone visiting any of the classrooms during the 16 weeks of clay activities probably would first have noticed the amount of verbalization which was occurring around tables where children were working with clay. One of the phenomena concerning children and clay is the amount of language it elicits. Because language of the young child is directly related to the readiness for reading and the ability to process classroom procedures (such as directions); because language is the basic means of communication expected from the child who enters school, it was important to learn if clay activities as provided in the Clay Project would influence children's verbal development.

Two tests used in the pre and posttesting period were particularly indicative of the effect of clay activities on verbal development. Clay Verbs was a test designed to evaluate the comprehension and vocabulary development. Each child was given two blocks of clay somewhat rectangular in shape. The person giving the test asked the child to do a series of actions with the clay, from the simplest "roll the clay" to the more complex "texturize the clay." Nineteen actions were asked during the test. (See the Appendix for a copy of the Clay Verbs Test). The other verbal test looked at the child's verbal enumeration of what parts can be found in either a dog or a person. By comparing which parts also appeared in the same child's clay dog or person, the child's understanding of the concept of what parts belong to a dog or a person can be better evaluated. It is assumed that the more parts which appear both in the clay piece and in the verbal enumeration, the stronger and more complete the child's concept of the subject. Listed as the Duplicates Test in Table 5, this test used data from the Verbal Enumeration Test, which can be found in the Appendix.

Results of the Clay Verbs Test

When the experimental cluster is compared with the Control Group, some interesting results can be found. Significant gains were made in both the experimental groups and the Control Group in regard to the understanding of clay verbs. While the Control Group children started at a lower level, and did not make as much of a gain, the experimental cluster children began somewhat higher and gained more. Age and maturation evidently influences the ability of young children at these ages to understand verbs. This is supported by the finding that kindergarten children in both the experimental cluster and the Control Group made significant gains, whereas only the pre-kindergarten children in the experimental cluster were able to indicate growth in their understanding of verbs. Boys and girls made similar gains, although boys in the Control Group made significant gains in Clay Verbs when compared to the girls in that group.

The Technique Group children made the greatest achievement levels in Clay Verbs. In fact, this group was the only one which showed improvement for Clay Verbs in both prekindergarten and kindergarten grades. The Encouragement Group had gains in pre-kindergarten but not kindergarten, and Discussion Group children did not show any progress at either level. The various strategies used by classroom teachers for each of the experimental groups reveals clues as to why the results came out as they did on this test. In Encouragement classrooms, teachers focused on supporting the child and describing whatever he or she was doing with the clay. This type of reinforcement and verbalization of the child's action may account for the improvement shown by children in this particular group. Discussion Group teachers communicated more about the concepts involved in a particular subject being taught, and gave no technical assistance. There was not as much talk about what the child was doing: instead of saying "look how you are rolling that dog's leg," the teacher might say in this group, "how many legs does the dog have?" In the Technique Group, teachers tried to emphasize "doing;" this tied directly to the strategy of helping children learn to deal directly with the clay medium itself through demonstrations. More emphasis on what was possible once the clay medium itself was understood led to much of the language which children needed to know to do well on the Clay Verbs Test. Examples were building the clay higher, smoothing the clay, carving the clay, and texturizing the clay.

Results of the Duplicates Test

Children in the experimental cluster were able to show more growth than those in the Control Group regarding the expression of the same concept in a verbal and a nonverbal medium. The difference was especially noticeable within the two prekindergarten groups; those four-year-olds who were in a group which utilized one of the teaching strategies made significantly higher gains than the Control Group children of the same age.

In the Technique Group, both prekindergarten and kindergarten children made strong gains, and, to a lesser extent, so did the children in the Discussion Group. The Encouragement Group and Control

Group children did not show growth. Looking at the differences between boys and girls, only the Technique Group showed significant gains for both. Encouragement Group girls made gains, but not the boys; Discussion Group boys made gains, but not the girls; in the Control Group, neither made progress.

Again, these findings support the theory that the more systems of the child in which intervention occurs, the better the concept development and the more complete and consistent the child's representation of that concept across media.

Table 5 shows the results of all the Verbal Cognitive Tests, including both the Clay Verbs Test and the Duplicates Test. The table is organized so that data from each of the three teaching strategies and the Control Group can be compared.

TABLE 5   ACHIEVEMENT OF PREKINDERGARTEN AND KINDERGARTEN CHILDREN IN EACH TEACHING PROGRAM ON VERBAL COGNITIVE TESTS

Cognitive/ Verbal Tests	Pretest		Posttest		Mean Gain	Sig. of Gain
	Mean	S.D.	Mean	S.D.	Gain	Gain
	ENCOURAGEMENT GROUP — PREKINDERGARTEN (N = 39)					
Clay Verbs	8.23	2.81	10.10	2.30	1.87	.01
Duplicates	3.58	2.61	5.27	3.03	1.69	*
Harris-Goodenough	74.82	12.75	80.92	12.51	5.50	.05
WPPSI Verbal I.Q.	91.31	11.52	91.08	10.35	5.77	.05
Information	7.80	2.41	0.03	2.84	1.23	.05
Vocabulary	8.13	2.39	8.23	1.86	.10	*
Arithmetic	9.26	2.07	10.10	1.89	.85	*
Similarities	10.00	3.40	11.05	2.91	1.05	
Comprehension	8.33	2.77	9.23	2.49	.90	

TABLE 5 (cont.)

Cognitive/ Verbal Tests	Pretest		Posttest		Mean Gain	Sig. of Gain
	Mean	S.D.	Mean	S.D.		
ENCOURAGEMENT GROUP – KINDERGARTEN (N = 42)						
Clay Verbs	10.93	2.65	11.83	2.12	.91	*
Duplicates	6.36	3.19	8.00	3.55	1.64	*
Harris-Goodenough	78.57	11.42	85.52	11.19	6.95	.05
WPPSI Verbal I.Q.	94.95	14.35	99.00	14.26	4.05	*
Information	8.69	2.93	9.57	2.93	.88	*
Vocabulary	8.19	2,86	8.88	2.56	.69	*
Arithmetic	9.62	2.71	9.45	2.20	.17	*
Similarities	10.26	3.03	11.10	3.20	.83	*
Comprehension	9.24	3.02	10.41	3.49	1.17	.05
DISCUSSION GROUP – PREKINDERGARTEN (N = 44)						
Clay Verbs	9.00	3.07	9.89	2.62	.89	*
Duplicates	4.30	2.96	6.07	4.01	1.78	.05
Harris-Goodenough	77.36	14.46	80.00	10.49	2.57	*
WPPSI Verbal I.Q.			95.73	11.49		
Information			9.21	2.72		
Vocabulary			7.96	2.05		
Arithmetic			9.80	2.23		
Similarities			10.71	3.06		
Comprehension			8.91	2.60		

TABLE 5 (cont.)

Cognitive/ Verbal Tests	Pretest		Posttest		Mean Gain	Sig. of Gain
	Mean	S.D.	Mean	S.D.		
DISCUSSION GROUP – KINDERGARTEN (N = 38)						
Clay Verbs	11.05	2.24	11.68	2.21	.53	*
Duplicates	5.96	2.35	8.16	3.52	2.20	.05
Harris-Goodenough	79.10	13.83	87.08	9.79	7.74	.01
WPPSI Verbal I.Q.			94.97	10.49		
Information			9.39	2.30		
Vocabulary			8.54	1.78		
Arithmetic			8.49	2.21		
Similarties			10.33	2.29		
Comprehension			9.59	2.75		
TECHNIQUE GROUP – PREKINDERGARTEN (N = 40)						
Clay Verbs	6.97	3.03	10.75	3.18	3.79	.001
Duplicates	2.72	2.95	6.16	3.85	3.44	.001
Harris-Goodenough	73.34	13.99	78.98	11.31	5.61	.05
WPPSI Verbal I.Q.	84.25	10.58	93.48	11.03	9.23	.001
Information	6.85	1.76	8.55	1.91	1.70	.01
Vocabulary	6.58	2.09	7.85	2.11	1.28	.05
Arithmetic	8.45	2.70	9.50	1.99	1.05	*
Similarities	8.65	2.91	9.98	3.34	1.33	*
Comprehension	7.08	2.33	9.85	2.73	1.98	.01
TECHNIQUE GROUP – KINDERGARTEN (N = 45)						
Clay Verbs	10.27	3.19	13.60	2.33	3.33	.001
Duplicates	6.81	4.20	9.15	4.31	2.35	.05
Harris-Goodenough	82.02	11.73	89.87	11.50	7.84	.01

TABLE 5 (cont.)

Cognitive/ Verbal Tests	Pretest		Posttest		Mean Gain	Sig. of Gain
	Mean	S.D.	Mean	S.D.		
	TECHNIQUE GROUP – KINDERGARTEN (N = 45) (cont.)					
WPPSI Verbal I.Q.	97.13	13.19	105.09	13.60	7.82	.001
Information	9.62	3.03	11.36	2.62	1.73	.01
Vocabulary	8.64	2.71	10.27	3.24	1.62	.01
Arithmetic	9.69	2.46	9.62	2.75	– .07	*
Similarities	10.20	2.89	11.62	3.07	1.42	.05
Comprehension	9.64	2.45	11.13	2.67	1.49	.05
	CONTROL GROUP – PREKINDERGARTEN (N = 39)					
Clay Verbs	8.36	2.50	9.31	2.81	.95	*
Duplicates	3.80	2.97	4.60	3.14	.80	*
Harris-Goodenough	79.00	13.21	80.69	9.83	1.63	*
WPPSI Verbal I.Q.	92.13	14.15	95.44	13.11	3.31	*
Information	8.31	2.54	8.56	2.79	.26	*
Vocabulary	7.54	2.42	8.72	2.41	1.18	.05
Arithmetic	9.54	3.25	9.82	2.36	.28	*
Similarities	10.36	3.38	10.64	3.27	.28	*
Comprehension	8.13	2.91	9.00	2.64	.87	*
	CONTROL GROUP – KINDERGARTEN (N = 38)					
Clay Verbs	9.82	2.38	11.84	2.58	2.03	.01
Duplicates	6.21	2.90	8.04	3.32	1.83	*
Harris-Goodenough	81.50	10.74	84.13	12.56	2.63	*
WPPSI Verbal I.Q.	93.95	14.00	96.00	13.78	2.05	*
Information	9.24	2.93	10.18	3.02	.95	*
Vocabulary	8.37	2.35	8.18	2.10	– .18	*
Arithmetic	9.71	2.89	9.32	2.67	– .40	*
Similarities	9.63	3.11	9.90	3.23	.26	
Comprehension	8.32	2.65	9.63	2.69	1.32	.05

No Significant Gain

III. The Influence of Clay Activities on Children's IQ

Although many educators would debate the validity of IQ tests and their application to educational practices, IQ tests are utilized by most school systems to some extent. Reporting on findings from two types of IQ tests which were used by the Clay Project for pre and posttesting will provide information which, when added to findings from other tests, may offer a more complete picture of the influence of clay activities on children's development.

Children at ages four and five have limited skills regarding verbalization, and certainly cannot be expected to take the types of tests designed for those with reading and writing abilities. Tests which are designed for very young children and which "get at" intelligence are few in number. Because of the ages of the children involved in the Clay Project, and due to the type of activities involved (clay and language skills, for example), both verbal and nonverbal areas of intelligence needed to be examined. Therefore, two tests were chosen which could provide information about a young child's intelligence as revealed in several media.

One of these tests is the Harris-Goodenough Drawing Test, a standardized IQ test that uses in its evaluation of drawing many of the same areas used in the evaluation of the cognitive achievement in clay, i.e., physical details, decorative details, correctly placed details, proportions, etc. The Harris-Goodenough Drawing Test evaluates only person drawings. Children were asked to draw both a dog and a person at separate times during the pre and posttesting to answer the question: If intervention occurs in one nonverbal medium (clay), will the child also improve in another nonverbal medium (drawing)?

The other intelligence test was the Wechsler Preschool Primary Scale of Intelligence (WPPSI). This is an individual intelligence test with various subtests and a total Verbal IQ score. In the school setting, the WPPSI testing package would usually be given and scored by a trained person such as a school counselor or psychologist. Charlotte Huddle, the elementary counselor on the staff of the Clay Project, trained teacher-testers to do the WPPSI during the pre and posttesting periods. She did the scoring of the results of the testing package. A problem which resulted from the administration of the WPPSI in the Discussion Group during the pretesting caused those findings to be unusable. Table 5, therefore, indicates the WPPSI findings for Encouragement, Technique and the Control Group, along with the results of the Harris-Goodenough for all three teaching strategies and the Control Group.

Results of the Harris-Goodenough Drawing Test

When the drawings of a person done by children during the pre and posttesting were evaluated using the Harris-Goodenough Drawing Test, the total experimental group and the Control Group children were compared. Although drawing is a different way of expression than clay (one being two-dimensional, the other three-dimensional, for example), by using similar means of evaluation it was possible to see if intervention in one medium would influence achievement in the other. Since the children in the Control Group made no significant improvement in drawing (despite the fact that they started in the pretest with higher mean scores), and the children in the various teaching strategies using clay in the classroom did improve in drawing, there was a definite transfer from one medium to the other.

Both prekindergarten and kindergarten children made greater gains in drawing in direct relationship to the number of systems in which teachers intervened. Kindergarten children made more transfer from clay activities to drawing than did prekindergarten children in the experimental cluster. Boys and girls both gained significantly in drawing abilities. Girls in the experimental cluster,

94

for example, scored five more points than the girls in the Control Group. As results from other Clay Project tests have indicated, without some kind of teaching strategy being used, girls made little improvement. This proved to be true in drawing as well. Boys, however, made gains in the nonverbal media of both clay and drawing even without intervention, but made greater gains in those classrooms where a teaching strategy was used.

Girls in the Encouragement Group made the most significant improvement in drawing, a gain of eight points. For the boys, the Technique Group proved the most successful (an 8.5 gain), compared to 5.6 for the Discussion boys and 3.7 for the Control Group boys. It is worth noting that girls seemed to do best in the program with the least structured intervention, Encouragement, whereas boys, who gained in every group, grew the most in drawing skills in the Technique Group.

Overall, the Technique Group children had the highest mean posttest scores and the largest gains. Differences in drawing achievement as measured by this scale appear to be more related to age and sex within groups. Prekindergarten children, for example, moved ahead 5.61 points in IQ as measured by the Harris-Goodenough scale, compared to 7.84 points for kindergarten children. All teaching programs were able to produce growth in drawing, all greater than the Control Group. (See Table 5) It would be possible to explain the progress in drawing made by Control Group children, although it was not significant, as due to the traditional use of drawing as part of the curriculum in most prekindergarten and kindergarten classrooms.

In summary, findings from the Harris-Goodenough Drawing Test indicate that if children are able to use a certain medium in a structured program, and learn certain concepts and skills in that medium, when they own those concepts or skills they can use them while expressing themselves in another medium. Drawing was not taught during the 16 week intervention period, but because children in the experimental cluster improved in clay skills and learned through that particular medium, they were also able to express what they had learned in drawing.

The verbal part of the WPPSI (the performance section was not utilized by the Clay Project) contains subtests as well as a Verbal IQ result. The subtests which might have particular application to classroom situations and teachers are:

Verbal IQ
    Information
    Vocabulary
    Arithmetic
    Similarities
    Comprehension

The experimental cluster children made significant gains in all WPPSI subtests except Arithmetic, while the Control Group children improved only in Comprehension. The experimental cluster children made a gain of over six points in Verbal IQ. The greatest difference between the groups was in Similarities, considered to be one of the better measurements of intelligence.

Prekindergarten children tended to gain slightly more than the kindergarten children in verbal cognition. Prekindergarten children improved in all subtests, while kindergarteners gained in three out of five subtests. It should be noted that although prekindergarten children's clay products did not reveal the level of development in integration of concepts shown by those made by kindergarteners, the prekindergarteners were clearly able to make improvments in verbal and cognitive skills. Clay seems especially valuable to younger children whose verbal ability may not enable them to express what they know. Without access to a nonverbal medium, they could show very little cognitive growth, or even lose, as was indicated by the Control boys.

A similar pattern related to boys and girls as was shown in other cognitive tests can be found in the WPPSI. Experimental cluster boys and girls both made significant gains, for example, in Verbal IQ. Control boys also gained, but Control Group girls made almost no improvement in any WPPSI subtest. Again, indicating the importance clay can have for boys in the early childhood classroom, Control boys improved enough in Verbal IQ so that the difference between the experimental cluster and Control Group boys was not significant.

TABLE 6   ACHIEVEMENT OF EXPERIMENTAL AND
                CONTROL GROUPS BY SEX ON WPPSI VERBAL I.Q.
                         AND SUBTESTS

WPPSI Subtests	Pretest		Posttest		Mean Gain	Sig. of Gain
	Mean Gain	S.D.	Mean Gain	S.D.		
EXPERIMENTAL BOYS (N = 83)						
Verbal I.Q.	90.18	13.40	98.04	14.39	7.87	.001
Information	7.81	2.63	9.30	3.10	1.49	.01
Vocabulary	7.48	2.70	8.78	2.76	1.30	.04
Arithmetic	9.27	2.67	9.56	2.50	.29	*
Similarities	9.44	3.17	10.64	3.29	1.19	.05
Comprehension	8.35	2.78	10.13	9.80	1.78	.01
EXPERIMENTAL GIRLS (N = 83)						
Verbal I.Q.	94.04	13.14	99.62	11.66	4.39	.01
Information	8.77	2.85	10.06	2.44	1.28	.01
Vocabulary	8.34	2.50	8.93	2.60	.59	*
Arithmetic	9.27	2.39	9.76	2.00	.49	*
Similarities	10.14	3.07	11.27	3.02	1.13	.05
Comprehension	7.50	2.45	9.87	2.69	.98	.05

TABLE 6 (cont.)

	CONTROL BOYS (N = 37)					
Verbal I.Q.	93.54	12.58	98.19	12.43	4.65	.05
Information	8.97	2.82	9.92	3.15	.95	*
Vocabulary	7.78	2.66	8.81	2.21	1.03	*
Arithmetic	9.92	2.83	9.92	2.18	.00	*
Similarities	10.03	2.83	10.84	2.87	.81	*
Comprehension	8.10	2.80	9.70	2.43	1.60	.01
	CONTROL GIRLS (N = 40)					
Verbal I.Q.	92.56	15.31	93.43	13.92	.88	*
Information	8.58	2.72	8.85	2.80	.28	*
Vocabulary	8.10	2.17	8.13	2.29	.03	*
Arithmetic	9.35	3.27	9.25	2.78	- .10	*
Similarities	9.98	2.63	9.75	3.52	.23	*
Comprehension	8.33	2.78	8.95	2.85	.63	*

* No Significant Gain

Children who took part in the Technique teaching strategy began at the lowest level and progressed farther than any other group. They had an 8.5 gain in Verbal IQ (compare this to the gains made by the Technique Group as revealed by the Harris-Goodenough Drawing Test; there is a striking similarity). The Technique Group children were the only ones to improve in Vocabulary and Similarities. The Encouragement Group children began at the same level as the Control Group, but made 4.9 points of gain compared to 2.7 points by the Control Group children. Overall, the WPPSI results follow closely those of the Harris-Goodenough test. (See Table 5)

98

To summarize, although intervention was in clay sculpturing, children improved in their ability or achievement on standardized IQ tests, performance and verbal (the Harris-Goodenough and the WPPSI), as well as in the medium of clay itself. Therefore, there is reaffirmation that if a child improves through a nonverbal medium, he or she improves in the ability to express that growth in a verbal medium as well.

IV. The Influence of Clay Activities on Children's Drawing

An additional method of evaluation was used by the Clay Project staff to examine the potential for transfer from a nonverbal to a verbal medium. The Drawing Observation Scale was developed by the staff to evaluate the person and dog drawings done by children during the pre and posttesting. (See Appendix for sample test). In addition to a written record of the process used by the child as the drawing was done, the test included a checklist of verbal activities of the child during drawing, the child's methods of drawing, how the child seemed to feel about drawing, and a section concerning the end result of the drawing itself. The drawing in the second part of the Drawing Observation Scale was evaluated according to:

Recognizability
Physical Details
Decorative Details
Background Details
Correctly Placed Details
Proportions
Perspective
Size of Drawing

The third section of the scale looked at the drawing techniques utilized by the child.

In the Drawing Observation Scale, all groups, including the Control Group, made significant gains in drawing achievement in the cognitive areas when the scores of the person and dog drawing were combined. In the subtests which assessed the details of the drawing and the technique, there were no significant differences between the Experimental Group and the Control Group. The two subtests which looked at Perspective and Proportion showed that the experimental cluster children indicated strong growth when compared with the Control Group children.

Similar results to those found in the Harris-Goodenough Drawing Test can be seen from the comparison of prekindergarten and kindergarten children using the Drawing Observation Scale. Older children who had intervention in clay activities made gains in drawing. Younger children seemed to learn what they were taught but made less transfer. Prekindergarteners did improve significantly in Perspective, suggesting that they were able to improve in their ability to perceive and express the relationships within the dimension of their surrounding environments.

As was true with the Harris-Goodenough Test, both boys and girls made gains in all groups. In each tested program, girls began with higher pretest scores than boys. Control Group boys and girls started and ended almost alike. Girls in the three experimental groups made higher posttest means than boys in the three groups, but because they had started with higher mean scores, their gains were not statistically significant. Girls in the Technique Group made the strongest growth when compared to all other groups.

All teaching programs made similar gains overall, all greater than the Control Group. For most children, the Technique Group was able to show the greatest improvement, having the highest mean posttest scores. The Technique Group children made the greatest improvement in Physical Details and Proportion. Results of the Drawing Observation Scale (from six subtests) can be found in Table 6. This table summarizes the four main areas which were tested (Cognitive Clay, Sculptural Clay, Drawing and Verbal Cognitive). For the Drawing Observation Scale results, the effect of teaching programs was not significant, but the pattern of growth can be found in each of the three teaching strategies despite no drawing being part of the Clay Project. As was mentioned earlier in this chapter, most prekindergarten and kindergarten children

100

are exposed to drawing, therefore, growth in drawing skills in the Control Groups is to be expected.

In conclusion, findings from the Drawing Observation Scale further support what was found in the Harris-Goodenough Drawing Test: The improvement in clay abilities has direct correlation to improvement in drawing abilites. Children were able to transfer what they learned in one nonverbal medium into another nonverbal medium.

V. Applications for Classroom Settings

In almost every test used to evaluate any changes in children's cognitive and artistic growth, the findings clearly support giving children as full a program of structured learning through clay activities as possible.

Children can be offered opportunities for clay activities in a supportive atmosphere, with time to better understand themselves and their world through their own explorations and trial and error efforts. These children can grow, as a result, in their cognitive clay capabilities, sculptural skills, and IQ. Further, they are able to transfer their gains to two other means of communicating, verbally and through drawing.

If, in addition, children are stimulated cognitively through ongoing observations and discussions related to their clay activities, they improve even more in their ability to learn through clay. By owning more of the concept, which occurs when children have chances to develop their perceptual and verbal skills, children can express more about their world.

When assistance in dealing with the medium of clay itself is provided along with the supportive atmosphere and the cognitive stimulation, children are able to indicate the most dramatic changes in their cognitive clay capabilities, sculptural skills, IQ, verbal abilities and drawing levels. Helping children discover ways to make the clay respond to ideas, while continuing to encourage verbalization,

101

observation, and discovery, is the most effective strategy for helping children learn.

TABLE 7 SIGNIFICANCE OF THE GAINS OF EACH TEACHING
PROGRAM AND THE SIGNIFICANCE OF THE EFFECT
OF PROGRAMS ON THE ACHIEVEMENT OF CHILDREN
IN CLAY, DRAWING, VERBAL COGNITION

Test and Subtests	Significance of the Gains				Sign.**of Effect of Teaching Programs
	Encourage.	Discuss.	Technique	Control	
Cognitive Clay	(N = 81)	(N = 83)	(N = 85)	(N = 77)	
Recogn.	.05	.001	.001	*	.001
Physical Det.	.001	.052	.001	*	.001
Correctly Pl.	.01	*	.001	*	.001
Proportions	.001	.001	.001	.05	.001
3-Dimensional	*	.001	.001	.05	.001
Whole Figure	*	*	.001	*	.001
Technique	.05	.001	.001	.05	.001
Sculptural Clay					
Overall	.05	.01	.001	*	.001
Surface	*	*	.01	*	.001
Space	*	.01	.01	*	.001
Unity	.05	.01	.01	*	.001
Expression	.01	.01	.01	*	.001
Utility	.01	.01	.01	*	.001
Average	.01	.01	.01	*	.001

102

TABLE 7 (cont.)

Drawing					
Recogn.	.001	.001	.001	.001	*
Physcial Det.	.001	.01	.001	.001	.077
Correctly Pl.	.001	*	.001	.001	.020
Proportions	.001	.001	.001	.001	.026
Perspective	*	*	.05	*	.022
Technique	.001	.001	.001	.001	*
Verbal Cognitve					
Clay Verbs	.01	*	.01	.01	.001
Duplicates	*	*	*	*	*
Harris-Good.	.01	.01	.01	*	.098
WPPSI I.Q.	.01		.01	*	.001
Information	.01		.01	*	.007
Vocabulary	*		.01	*	.001
Arithmetic	*		*	*	*
Similarities	*		.01	*	.001
Comprehension	.05		.01	.01	.001

* No Significant Gain
** Analysis of Variance Considering Group, Grade, Sex

Table 7 summarizes the findings from each of the Clay Project's three teaching strategies, as well as the Control Group. The level of significant growth indicated in almost every test and subtest clearly shows the Technique teaching strategy, which intervened in the most systems of the child, was able to help children grow in their abilities more effectively than the other strategies.

103

Just as no two children respond to clay activities in exactly the same way, so no two teachers will utilize clay in their classrooms in an identical fashion. Teachers need to feel able to experiment in their classroom using the findings of the Clay Project as guides. In some classrooms, it may seem appropriate, for several reasons, to offer an encouragement type of program using clay. Interest centers might be set up which would include clay; plenty of time for children to use clay in the center would still result in some artistic and cognitive growth. Additional growth would result from providing clay activities once or twice a week in a structured program which includes observation and discussion of ideas children can express in clay. By teaming with an art resource person or art teacher, classroom teachers with less background in art methods can still add the extra dimension which comes when children learn ways to utilize clay effectively. When added to the supportive, structured program of regularly scheduled clay activities, this approach will help the most children in the most effective way.

Many teachers have discovered that for them, using a blend of all the teaching strategies during the school year works well. There may be particular projects or events which seem to lend themselves to the more technical approach, while at other times, simply providing time, clay and encouragement is enough. The findings show that girls in particular may need plenty of encouragement to get started; however, once familiar with the clay and the possible outcomes, many girls may be ready for other strategies. Boys, as the results indicated, benefit greatly from clay activities. The fact that boys can gain in cognitive and sculptural skills even with little or no intervention means that clay is a natural learning tool which teachers can utilize to assist boys, in particular, in the school setting.

Further research studies utilizing the arts as a medium for learning should be undertaken, particularly regarding teaching children with language differences, including dialectic variations, second language learning, and speech and language deficiencies. Through the non-verbal media of clay, drawing and sociodramatic play, children can express concepts and develop ideas which do not depend upon an area of possible weakness, language. Over a period of time, as the concepts become fully "owned" by the child, the research indicates that children are able to transfer their learning into other areas. Therefore, the child who is able to express ideas through clay or drawing may eventually be able to express them through language as well. The research conducted in both the United States and Israel indicates that the clay medium itself was productive for developing language. This was due partly to the free-flowing exchange of ideas which seem to occur naturally around a table of children involved in clay activities. Even prekindergarten children were able to extend their language capabilities when they were exposed to clay in some type of ongoing program. When their experiences were enriched, so were their vocabularies.

Since the conclusion of the original study, research staff members and teachers have continued to use clay utilizing one or more of the teaching strategies. Children from widely differing backgrounds and of varying ages have been exposed to the "clay as a learning tool" idea. Whether it is a one-time demonstration for teachers, a series of clay sessions with children in a YMCA, an international group of students in a school in Hong Kong, or a remedial reading class of upper grade level children, features from the original study have been utilized and findings reconfirmed.

Clay is intriguing: it is fascinating to feel,
to shape, to explore. It can be manipulated;
the same object can be made and remade in
many variations without the penalities of
starting over associated with paper/pencil
activities.

Clay increases language: there is a natural
flow of talk around a table of children making
objects with clay. Also, clay lends itself
to such verbal areas as verbs, generalizations,
comparisons, measurements, descriptions, etc.

Clay reduces tensions: the emotional levels
sometimes associated with more troublesome
members of a group can often be lessened

through an absorbing clay lesson. Some children who rarely participate in other activities,
and seldom produce anything, are able to do so
through the medium of clay.

Clay is an open-ended medium: in the extended
weeks of the clay research, children never
tired of the clay and seldom ran out of ideas,
even when not provided with topics by the
teacher.

Even the most skeptical administrator, if shown the data from the
Clay Project, would find it difficult to deny the effectiveness of using
clay in the classroom to help children learn. From such a humble
material can come a wealth of benefits for children, and, therefore,
for teachers as well.

5

CLAY: CHILDREN IN ACTION

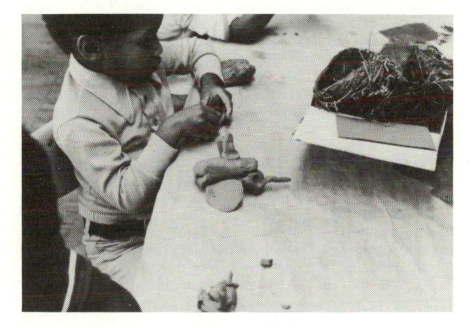

The research conducted by the Clay Project indicates that teachers often must go beyond providing support and encouragement if children are to increase their cognitive and artistic skills. In the promotion of learning through the medium of clay, all three teaching strategies, encouragement, observation/discussion, and technique, can effectively be utilized by teachers. These three approaches, used separately or together, can dramatically help children in the development of learning skills in cognitive as well as affective areas. As described in Chapter Three, each of the teaching strategies can be appropriate in particular settings and for certain situations. Just as in other areas of the curriculum, such as reading, teachers adapt approaches to fit the needs and interests of clusters of children within the total class, so can teachers do the same within the framework of an art lesson. The criteria is what works best for children, as well as what teachers are able to do. Thus, for a certain group, words of encouragement spoken periodically throughout a clay lesson may be all that is needed; for another number of children, instruction about specific techniques might be helpful.

Making decisions about when to offer more direction and how much is appropriate can be difficult, especially for less experienced teachers. Those teachers who have worked with a particular age group of children over a period of time can more readily transfer understanding of certain behaviors and needs indicated by children from one context to another. For example, the child who has the habit of not listening to directions may not listen during instructions for an art lesson; the child who hurries through a task may need as much slowing down in working with clay as with arithmetic problems. Both experienced and beginning teachers may be equally challenged by the requirements of teaching with a medium such as clay. Few teachers have had opportunities to use clay in an ongoing classroom program. Little is understood about the medium itself or how children respond to and use it as a tool for learning. Before teachers can expect children to fully benefit from clay in the classroom, teachers themselves must experience the rewards and frustrations, the excitement and challenge, of creating with this amazing medium. Once teachers have gained experience with clay, both personally and in their teaching, an awareness can begin to develop concerning the instructional approach which best fits a particular need and setting. As in other areas of instruction, timing is important. Knowing when just a few words will make a difference, and what words to use; understanding when a child is ready for more technical information and how much; realizing that a few students need to watch a demonstration one more time: these are all examples of teaching strategies which can make the difference between *hoping* that children will learn and *planning* in order that they will learn.

Dr. Ross Mooney, who worked with the original Clay Project staff as a consultant, was for many years a member of the Department of Educational Development at The Ohio State University. One of Mooney's interests for many years has been the child as a creator. According to Mooney, children must give some type of response whenever they are expected to react to a stimulus:

> The principle which appears to govern the effectiveness of a method in respect to stimulus and response is that children prosper best when what they receive as stimulus is balanced out by what they are then capable to give as their response.
>
> The stimulus can be increased in its range of complexity as response increases in its range of capability to handle complexity. A response fully formed in balance with its stimulus is invitation, then, to increase the range of the stimulus; thus growth occurs.
>
> (Mooney, 1973)

What Mooney is saying fits into the idea of utilizing a multi-level approach to teaching with clay. Knowing which children are ready for more complex stimuli, and what kinds of responses children should be able to give are vital for any teaching in all parts of the curriculum. In regard to teaching with clay, there will be children capable of only simple, basic responses: the general shape of a bird with few or no details, for example. Other children may be ready to receive stimulation which could help them explore beyond the basic shapes, adding such areas as textures and details. Increasing the range of complexity of the stimuli without losing the important balance between the stimulus and the response demands that the teacher understand needs and interests of both a particular age group and the individual children within the classroom walls. Demands upon the child's intelligence and creativity should be in harmony with where an individual child happens to be relative to development, both cognitive and affective. Particularly with young children, changes between various levels of development and readiness can occur rapidly, sometimes within a single lesson. Clay, in a visible and concrete way, provides evidence of such changes, allowing teachers to become aware quickly that learning is happening. Since transfer of learning has been shown to occur between clay and such areas as vocabulary, it is possible to expect children to apply what they have learned in one context to another. Thus, if the child understands inside and outside as concepts during a clay lesson, those concepts should be understood in relationship to such areas as physical space (the classroom) or when used in a story read to the class. When teachers reinforce the transfer of concepts, deeper and more meaningful learning can result.

Up to this point, emphasis has been placed on the teaching approaches and their importance to helping the child grow cognitively and affectively. Although the previous chapter offers considerable data and statistics on what happened to groups of children because of clay, it is difficult to translate these facts and, figures into classrooms and individual children. In the remainder of this chapter, an attempt will be made to go behind the statistics and offer brief looks at some of the children who participated in the research or who have since become involved in the many programs based upon the research findings. By focusing on individual children, it may be possible to more fully understand the impact of clay activities on the learning process. The observation and evaluating of growth and change as revealed by a particular child might provide a better sense of how clay activities are able to make a difference.

Clay, when used in an ongoing, planned program, has been shown to make a significant impact upon young children's cognitive and affective development. In general, there are four areas, perceptual/motor, emotional, cognitive, and artistic/creative, in which children seem to develop skills through a program which utilizes clay as one of its basic media. No matter what the teaching strategy, each of these areas, to some extent, comes into play. While stress may be placed, for example, on cognitive skill development within a particular lesson, all other areas exist as well as the individual child makes an object with clay. There is no way to completely separate out one area from another. For the purposes of discussion, certain characteristics within a skill area will be delineated in this chapter, but with the understanding that these exist in tandem with other skills as well.

Developing Perceptual and Motor Skills

Tamera's black hair was braided into tiny rows all over her small head. With a sweet smile, made all the more delightful by several missing teeth, Tamera was eager to learn and seemed to enjoy her kindergarten class. Tamera's teacher quickly discovered that Tamera had had limited experience in such activities as cutting, pasting, and drawing. When asked to circle a picture, Tamera made awkward, irregular movements with the crayon or pencil. While it was clear that many of the problems would be taken care of by time and experience, the teacher realized that if Tamera began to feel her efforts were unsuccessful as she compared them with classmates, she might begin to lose her eagerness to learn and gradually have less confidence in herself. Clay activities were one way in which Tamera was able to have successful experiences despite her weak motor skills. Tamera found that the clay, unlike pencils or crayons, was very responsive to her small fingers and hands. Whereas the pencil, for example, sometimes wouldn't do quite what she wanted it to do, the clay was easy to mold into simple, interesting shapes. What Tamera didn't realize as she squeezed and kneaded the clay, and rolled and patted it into shapes, was that she was developing the necessary small and large muscles so that she could eventually have better control over the pencil and crayons.

While not all of the children in Tamera's class needed to improve motor skills to the same extent as did Tamera, all benefited from the

111

opportunity to increase in manual dexterity as the result of the demands of a clay program. As the lessons increase in complexity, so does the need for more control of the muscles, as well as hand-eye coordination. Putting ears and eyes on a clay dog requires more dexterity than shaping the dog's body. Particularly for younger children, activities involving use of both large and small muscles are important. Many children come to prekindergarten and kindergarten classes with poorly developed motor skills. Whereas children of earlier generations often spent much of their time engaged in a variety of physical activities, both indoors and outside, today's children are more likely to spend time indoors in less active pursuits, such as watching television. To attain the necessary motor skills needed for school-related tasks such as writing, cutting, and outlining, children need a variety of physical activities. Clay lessons, with their range of demands upon small and large muscles, as well as hand-eye coordination, can make a significant contribution toward helping children increase these skills.

Many children of four and five have had little experience in looking closely enough at objects which are around them so they can describe these objects, either verbally or nonverbally. Learning to focus attention on something for a long enough period of time to see that object clearly and in detail, may, for some children, require some kinds of planned activities during which they can gradually learn to see what they are looking at. Curtis, for example, was a preschooler who would glance quickly at something the teacher was showing the class, then move his attention to something else. It was also clear, from observing Curtis' drawing skills, that he had problems with hand-eye coordination. The skill needed to concentrate his attention on what he was doing was weak, so that both in regard to his perceptual ability and to his skill in communicating his ideas in visual forms, Curtis needed help.

An intensive program with clay provided Curtis with needed practice on observation and perception. When what he later would be making with clay depended upon his observation of something, Curtis discovered that he could spend the necessary time closely looking at that object. The teacher spent time helping Curtis discover more and more about what he was seeing. For example, when the class was about to make birds with clay, Curtis had previously spent time looking at pictures and models of birds. While looking at the pictures and models, the teacher asked Curtis questions about various details or aspects, and helped him to focus his attention on one part at a time. Starting out slowly, perhaps initially looking for one or two details, Curtis gradually increased his skills so that he could distinguish a number of details or particulars at once. His clay pieces began to reflect this same range of complexity, with more thought and expression being shown in the various products. Clay helped Curtis improve his ability to perceive and translate the world around him. Because he was expected to look closely at objects and then describe these, both in class discussions and in his clay pieces, Curtis began to focus his attention and to look for the overall form as well as the details.

Many of the activities utilized by preschool and primary classroom teachers help children to develop perceptual and motor skills. Drawing and painting, puzzles, games, etc., all can contribute to skill attainment in physical dexterity and perception. It is important to realize, however, that clay, as a three-dimensional media and as a flexible, responsive material, offers particularly broad and rich ways in which these skills can be fostered. In combination with other activities, clay makes a significant contribution to an area of development so necessary for future success in school and in life. The ability to concentrate upon and to see clearly what is being looked at, and then find ways to communicate a personal view of what has been seen through some means (words, drawing, clay), is vital to the process of learning.

Developing Emotional Strengths

Although bright and alert, four-year-old Andy was physically smaller than most children of his age, and quite shy. Around the clay table, however, Andy seem to blossom. At first, he spent much of his time exploring the texture and forming qualities of the medium; he pounded the clay, dug his fingernails into it, and pinched bits of clay between his fingers. After several sessions, Andy began to roll the clay; sometimes many tiny balls would begin to stack up around him on the table, or piles of pancake shapes would emerge. Over a period of weeks, Andy moved through several stages of development. He began to name shapes and add recognizable details. As he worked, Andy started to take more time to form the clay, smoothing parts or adding textures. Soon he was answering questions about his clay pieces from other children at his table. During sharing time, Andy proudly showed his clay objects and gave vivid descriptions of what various parts were for or what they did. It soon became apparent that Andy had a storytelling bent, and enjoyed making up stories about his clay pieces. At times, other children at his table joined him and the result was often an impromptu series of dramatic scenes with clay objects as the stars.

For Andy, clay was one medium through which he could express himself clearly and effectively. The recognition and praise he received both from his teacher and classmates increased his sense of self-worth and self-confidence. Andy's teacher noticed that some of the confidence gained by Andy during the clay periods seemed to be carrying over into other situations as well. He seemed more willing to speak up for himself rather than sitting back and allowing more aggressive children to assume leadership roles. Other children looked to Andy for ideas during other activities, remembering that during clay time Andy had been the one to suggest putting all the zoo animals together and then make cages for them; and that Andy had thought of a way to make tracks for the clay train everyone had helped construct.

For Andy, clay was an exciting medium of expression from the first day he began to work with it. Occasionally, however, there will be a child who initially regards clay with uncertainty. Nancy was sent to kindergarten each day wearing a spotlessly clean, usually frilly, dress. After observing Nancy during play and other active periods, her teacher realized that Nancy hung back when the other children were on the floor engaged in some project, and that she seemed unwilling to take her turn painting at the big easel. When the class prepared to work with clay, donning big shirts to protect clothes, Nancy still indicated reluctance to become involved. A phone call to

Nancy's mother revealed that Nancy was sent to school each day with the admonition to "keep clean!" When she realized that this restriction was preventing her daughter from entering into the various activities of the kindergarten class, Nancy's mother began to send her to school dressed more appropriately.

Once she discovered that clay did, in fact, wash off her hands and brush-off clothes, Nancy began to explore, tentatively at first, some of the possibilities. Her first efforts were brief and small in scale, but after a few weeks, Nancy's work in clay became more confident and expressive. Nancy's teacher realized that helping her discover the satisfaction and enjoyment to be found in creating with such materials as paint and clay was particularly important in Nancy's situation. It would be easy for a child to discover that it was possible to use the excuse that an activity was "messy" to avoid doing something which was new and therefore unknown, and that might not be done "right." While some children might require extra time to become familiar with a new situation or material, with encouragement and preparation they would be more willing and able to move into the unknown.

Clay activities helped Andy and Nancy both gain in self-confidence. For Andy, this was the result of recognition; for Nancy, because of her eventual overcoming of a psychological barrier. Both Andy and Nancy had several ways to communicate ideas to others, clay being one of these. For Som, however, clay and other nonverbal media were at first the only methods of sharing ideas. Som, a slight boy with big brown eyes, had recently come to the United States from Laos. Even at five years of age, Som had an understanding of the artistic expression which was part of his former country's culture. To the amazement of other children in the kindergarten class, Som was able, seemingly with little effort, to create beautifully crafted bowls, birds, animals and other shapes from the lumps of clay he was given. Som, who could speak almost no English, was able to communicate to his classrooms through this nonverbal medium. Drawn to Som as he created with the clay, the children made efforts to help break down the communication barrier by responding to what he was making. In the process, Som learned to speak some more words, and the children in the class realized, with the help of the teacher, that Som was able to utilize another language which was in itself rich and meaningful.

Developing a positive self-image and a means of meaningful self-expression are important for children, and can impact directly on success or lack of success in school. Particularly for those children who, for one reason or another, are unable to communicate effectively through the usual means of the spoken or written word, non-verbal media such as clay can be the door to gain enough confidence and experience so that, eventually, there is enough confidence to learn the other ways to communicate as well. A medium like clay can thus act as a bridge, allowing children opportunities to express ideas and feelings. Evidence of skills and intelligence can be provided which otherwise might take months to reveal. Such evidence can be used as the basis for many activities and expectations which the teacher can have ongoing in the classroom setting.

Clay activities fulfilled another type of need for Nick. Nick was an extremely active child, and had been diagnosed as having borderline hyperactivity. Constantly moving, Nick talked continually and could stay in his seat only for short periods of time. He had an extensive vocabulary for a five-year-old, and was obviously intelligent. Nick's teacher was apprehensive about including him in the clay activities, afraid that he would have difficulty restraining himself. She could visualize clay flying about the room. At first, Nick spent almost the entire clay period pounding and smashing the clay on the table, talking to himself. But to the teacher's surprise, Nick concentrated on the clay for 15 or 20 minutes at a time, longer than on any other activity she had observed him doing. In addition, he seemed calmed down after the time with the clay, and was able to listen to a story told to the class by the teacher without getting up and wandering around. It wasn't until the ninth or tenth session with clay that Nick decided to actually shape an object with the clay. Once he discovered that he could "make stuff", he began creating a series of monsters and creatures, each of which he named and about which he told stories. He continued to spend up to a half hour working with the clay each time, and seemed to be more relaxed and responsive afterwards.

116

Although it became obvious that Nick was increasing his cognitive and artistic skills after some weeks of working with the clay, what seemed to the teacher more significant were the gains he made in self-control. Nick himself seemed to realize that for him, the clay meant more than it did for other children. This was clarified for Nick's teacher when Nick arrived at school one morning and walked over to her, announcing "I need the clay, Mrs. Moore." Noticing how tightly-drawn Nick's face looked, Mrs. Moore quietly got out some of the earth clay from the covered container and handed it to him. Taking it over to a corner table, Nick began to hit and pound the clay over and over, muttering to himself "Bad clay, bad clay!" After about ten minutes, Nick calmly rolled the clay up into a ball and then returned it. For the rest of the morning, Nick played and worked happily with the class. What had caused Nick to ask for the clay that particular morning, Mrs. Moore never discovered. What was apparent, however, was that clay, for Nick, provided a release of tension and frustration, and allowed him to be more receptive of other kinds of learning and experiencing.

In many classrooms with several disruptive or overly-active children, teachers discovered that clay, instead of adding to the problems, could lessen them. When expectations were clearly stated and enforced, and such activities as getting out and putting away the clay were structured as part of the lesson, behavior problems were few. When children sensed that the teacher believed clay to be an important medium, one which offered opportunities for learning as well as for enjoyment, then they also tended to regard the clay times as valuable.

Developing Cognitive Skills

Angela was sitting at a table rolling out balls of clay, then carefully flattening each one. Her small nose wrinkled in concentration, Angela was humming quietly to herself as she worked. When the teacher smiled at her and encouraged her to talk about what she was doing, Angela explained that she was making breakfast and these were the pancakes. When the teacher asked if there would be enough so that each preschooler in the class could have one, Angela looked puzzled for a moment. Then with a delighted smile, she began to count the pancakes spread out before her. Angela's teacher was also delighted; up until this time, Angela had been one of the few children in the class who had not counted out loud to at least ten. As Angela continued to count, she hesitated several times once she passed the number ten. With a little help, she kept going, finally reaching the last pancake, number 19! Angela looked at the teacher and said, "There's 15 in our class, so you can have the rest." From this one brief experience, the teacher discovered that not only could Angela count, she could understand than 19 was more than 15.

The young child who arrives in first grade without the basic cognitive skills such as those required for counting and naming, will have a difficult time and will be unable to develop higher skills until the basic ones are mastered. If the child learns only by rote, and the concepts involved are not internalized and owned by that child, then the knowledge cannot be applied.

While most teachers clearly understand this situation and what is required, some still do not provide enough activities for young children which allow them to experience the learning and therefore, be able to fully understand it. Along with other materials, clay can be used to develop a program which permits children a full range of activities to go beyond memorization or copying. Its flexibility and adaptability allow clay to be used in an astonishingly diverse number of cognitively significant activities. The experience described in the example of Angela and the pancakes has many variations. Other types of lessons could involve acting out action verbs using people or animals of clay; learning about variations in sizes with clay shapes of any type; discovering volume (a long, skinny coil of clay takes as much clay as does a fat, square box), finding out about weight (why does the clay feel heavier when it's wet than it does when it's dry?). In addition, there are endless ways in which cognitive learning can occur when teachers incorporate the clay lesson into a total experience which includes gathering information about a particular subject before it is made during the clay period, sharing that information, discussing the results, etc.

118

Daniel, a four-year-old livewire in a busy preschool class, had been working with clay for about four weeks. The preschoolers were making bowls, and Daniel produced an almost flat piece of clay for his first attempt. The teacher asked Daniel, "Can your bowl hold some soup for me?" Daniel stared at his piece of clay and shook his head. Then the teacher reminded him about the bowls the class had seen earlier, and about the inside and outside parts. Using the piece of clay she had been holding in her hand as she walked around the room, the teacher demonstrated again for Daniel the basic pinchpot shape she had shown the class just before the clay had been distributed. "See if you can find a way to make a bowl can hold enough soup so that I can come back later and have some!"

The teacher watched from the other side of the room as Daniel looked around at the other bowls being made by his tablemates, and then back at his own piece of clay. He picked up his piece of clay and rolled it into a ball, then began shaping it by pressing his thumb, then his fingers, into the soft material. Gradually, a deep well was formed. When the teacher arrived after a few minutes, Daniel proudly offered her a taste of his "soup." In the process of making his bowl, Daniel had learned the concept of inside and outside. Because this concept had been experienced rather than explained, it was able to be internalized and become part of Daniel's understanding.

Sometimes an entire class can move forward in terms of cognitive growth because of an activity. Often, this type of activity occurs spontaneously, usually during a planned or structured lesson. In one kindergarten class, a stuffed bear named Henri had become almost a member of the class! (See cover) He accompanied students on field trips, ate with them during snack time, and listened to the stories told by the teacher. Henri was almost the same size as the smallest class member, and could be found sitting quietly in his chair watching as the children engaged in their clay lessons. One day, the teacher and the children decided it was Henri's birthday. During clay time, the children were to make bowls. Of course, the bowls that day would hold ice cream. Some children completed their bowls and decided to make a clay cake. Other children added candles, which led to the question of Henri's age. A counting lesson emerged to be sure there were enough candles. The teacher asked how many pieces of cake would be needed if everyone in the room was to have one, and more counting and checking took place. There was a lively discussion about how to cut the cake into equal pieces, and the solution did need a little help from the teacher. The children, however, did the actual dividing. The entire class, with Henri at the front of the room dressed in a party hat, happily sang a loud and enthusiastic "Happy Birthday to You!"

For this kindergarten class, the birthday party for Henri was a great deal of fun and resulted in many affective benefits. The learning which occurred, however, went beyond having a good time. Several mathematical principles and concepts were experienced, and the children understood through the processing of the necessary steps how to apply these concepts. Going beyond the explanation and copying methods, (such as using the "easy to find and distribute" dittoes), is essential if children, particularly those of preschool and primary ages, are to fully comprehend a concept. Also in the birthday clay experience was the opportunity to engage in a variety of actions which could be named, and which the teacher included in her observations and discussions that day ("You're doing a great job of *dividing* up the cake." "Jill, did you see how much *wider* this bowl is than this one?" "Show me how you made that so *smooth*!") Throughout the lesson, the children of the kindergarten class were engaging in visual discrimination, generalization and differentiating; they were developing their vocabularies and concepts of space. Because clay activities are so open to intellectual stimulation, both from the teacher and from one child to another, there is a constant, ongoing flow of both cognitive and affective aspects, each reinforcing and developing the other. Whereas in a paper/pencil type of activity, the children tend to be seated quietly, each expected to individually respond to questions or process information, a nonverbal medium such as clay offers another option, allowing children to engage in a *group* learning situation. For many children, the stimulation and the enjoyment provided by such an option makes the learning which occurs appear effortless. Perhaps this is one reason many teachers are skeptical that having an ongoing program of activities such as those proposed in this book can result in the increase of cognitive

120

abilities. How can anything which is so much fun teach children the basic skills which they need?

In any classroom, not all children will be ready to learn certain skills or ideas at the same time. Habu, a small, round black boy, was everyone's favorite. Almost always happy, Habu also was not eager to test his happy state by exerting himself in any direction. Instead, Habu was willing to let other people seek him out, which they did primarily because of his sweet disposition and his willingness to laugh at almost anything. He seemed quite willing to sit back and watch as the other children built with blocks, painted a mural, or shaped the clay. When encouraged, Habu would pick up something and manipulate it or look at it for a time, but usually paid more attention to what was going on around him than to what was is his hands.

During the clay lessons, it became obvious that Habu was fascinated by what the other children were making. He seemed to be listening intently during the introduction to each project; when the teacher asked him a specific question, such as which bowl was biggest in the story she had read about the *Three Bears*, Habu always knew the answer. When clay was placed in front of him, Habu would poke and pinch at it for a time, but made little effort to create a definite object. After about eight weeks of clay activities, the children were involved in creating objects using any ideas they wished. Many were remembering specific clay pieces they had made in the preceding weeks which seemed particularly successful, and were making variations of these. Since birds had been the most recently taught lesson, many children were shaping a bird, some with nests. Habu watched a friend next to him for a short time and then asked, "How do you make a bird?" The friend showed Habu how he was making his bird, and they talked about some of the things they had learned about birds. Habu turned to his clay and began, with quickness and determination, to shape a bird! Within the space of a few minutes, Habu had made a fairly accurate representation of a bird. He asked for more clay, and began a production-line of birds: birds hatching, birds in a nest, birds inside eggs, etc. Within that one period of time, Habu moved through several levels of clay development. He was "ready" for the process to assume meaning for him, and his time-clock had gone off.

121

The next clay time was also a free choice of subjects, and Habu decided the time had come to make a dog. First he asked the teacher to show him the pictures of dogs she had shown the class several weeks before when they were preparing to create dogs out of clay. By his comments, it was also clear that Habu remembered vividly the visit made by a dog and her puppies to the kindergarten class-room. Taking his clay in his hands, Habu proceeded to model his idea of a dog. In the succeeding weeks, Habu continued to work with the clay, eager to make whatever subject was suggested by the teacher. Each time, before he began, Habu paused for a moment, saying to himself, "Now let me think." The serious, intent look on his round face was such a contrast to his usual placid smile that the teacher felt she could almost read the mental process as it occurred. Habu, once he had decided he was ready, responded to the stimulus of the clay and the particular subject from his experience and with his growing cognitive and artistic abilities.

Cognitive growth spurts can occur within a group of children, each of whom acts as spark on the others during some kind of experience or activity. These interactions are usually spontaneous, although teachers sensitive to the interests and needs of children in the class can assist by orchestrating the various elements (such as materials and setting). In clay activities, one child might begin a chain of ideas with one small piece. In one kindergarten class, Markus made a cow, remembering the visit the class had made to a farm the previous week. Sara, sitting beside Markus, joined by making a mother pig and her piglets. Soon every child at the table was making an animal which had been seen at the farm, while at the same time talking animatedly about the various animals and the farm visit. The teacher stopped at their table and asked why no one was making lions and tigers. A lively discussion followed among the children about differences be-tween farm animals and zoo or wild animals. The eating habits and environments of the classes of animals was discussed, with the teacher providing information when asked. Several books in the classroom were used to clarify points and gather facts. While the discussion had been going on, Julie had been quietly making a farmer, his wife and two children. When the teacher asked her to explain what she was doing, the children were delighted. One child thought of the song *Farmer in the Dell* which the class had learned. Soon the entire class joined in singing, and several children made additional clay pieces to fit the various verses!

Beyond the pure enjoyment of the experience, children in this class gained both affectively and cognitively. Pulling out just a few examples: categorizing and differentiating (zoo animals compared to farm animals); generalizing (all animals have four legs); spatial understanding (seeing how an animal looked from all sides); transfering and interpreting ideas from one mode to another (verbalizing about farms and farm animals, making them in clay, singing about them); developing pride in personal expression as shown concretely in the clay pieces; increasing vocabulary words and understanding of these. From one small clay animal, an entire lesson grew, rich in its content and application to what children already knew and what additionally they could learn.

Developing Artistic Skills

Portia was a tall, attractive black girl in a large kindergarten class. The room was filled with things to see and do, and there was enough space for several activities to occur simultaneously. Portia loved to explore the various kinds of centers which the teacher had established, each with a somewhat different emphasis and with its own type of materials. The clay was included in one of the activity centers, and attracted Portia frequently. When the entire class participated in clay projects, Portia was one of the more creative students. She enjoyed finding her own solutions to the problems set by the teacher. When the class made bowls, for example, Portia made three, each decorated with a variety of designs. Portia's clay dog had a lease, a bowl, and a rug on which to sleep!

Because Portia was more advanced than many of her classmates in terms of her sensitivity to design, her skill at modeling, and her awareness of detail, her clay products seemed relatively sophisticated. To continue challenging a child like Portia required her teacher to enlist the aid of several resource people, including the art teacher who was in the building parttime, and a potter who lived near the school. From these people, the teacher learned to encourage Portia to take more time in completing her clay pieces; being more advanced allowed Portia to feel that her efforts, even when rushed and somewhat sloppy, were still "better" than those of other children. By seeing the work of older, more experienced artists, Portia was able to see that her pieces could be improved. The art teacher was glad to spend a little extra time with Portia, and she was able to help her try out a potter's wheel. For a child such as Portia, who is obviously ready for more advanced work and who seems to have a strong interest in a medium such as clay, having the opportunity to explore that medium in depth as a young child can have a significant impact on later career choices and/or avocations. Although few children will go on to become artists, there is always the possibility that more would be able to make that choice if given more opportunities to discover their affinity for art. Clay, which has tended to be a relatively ignored medium in many elementary and preschool classrooms, is a medium which permits those children who are particularly interested or capable of expression in three-dimensions to explore their own potential along with the clay.

While Portia may represent the exceptional child in the classroom, she is not unusual to the extent many educators might believe. Given the opportunity and the setting, many additional children could provide evidence of so-called giftedness in art expression. And since each child has a slightly different internal sense of timing as to when the particular stimulus received will be given a particular response, that child who has seemed up to a particular point in time to be average may suddenly give visible evidence that much more awareness and ability exists than was thought. As data from the clay project research indicates, many boys of preschool and early elementary ages are particularly able to benefit from an ongoing program in clay. It is not surprising, for example, to find a child like Teddy. At first, Teddy seemed to be so slow and careful in working with the clay that the teacher often had to cajole him into finishing after the others had begun cleaning up. Anxious that his clay pieces look like all the others at his table, Teddy seem to spend more time watching the other children make their clay pieces than he did on his own work. Over time, with encouragement from the teacher, Teddy began to feel more comfortable about experimenting with the clay, and wasn't so concerned about his pieces resembling others. One reason for the lessening of concern was the discovery that clay was flexible enough to allow him to change his ideas without being penalized. Finally, Teddy began to get so caught up in what he was creating that he forgot for minutes at a time the other children were making clay pieces; he was able to enter the act of creation and allow it to take precedence. His clay pieces began to reveal his own personality and eye for detail. The clay was able to tap in Teddy a well of creativity which the teacher had no idea existed in him. Because he was given sufficient time to develop his interest, Teddy moved beyond the initial awkwardness and hesitation, which, if there had only been one or two clay lessons, would have marked him as one of the less creative children in the class.

It is difficult for adults to view art works of young children without making comparisons with adult art, but as much as possible, children's art should stand on its own merits. While clay pieces made by four and five-year-olds may seem crude and without aesthetic interest to adults, a closer look reveals that children's work in clay can be both original and expressive. Four-year-olds may lack the manual dexterity to form intricate or sophisticated products, but can make fresh and delightful interpretations of their worlds. Jessica, a Chinese-American six-year-old, created a table and a complete set of dishes to go on top of the table. Each bit of clay was shaped to resemble a particular type of container, and time was spent placing tiny designs around edges. Jessica based her ideas on her kitchen table at home, and the freshness of her interpretation was evident in the way in which she put together the various elements. Instead of looking stiff and finished, the pieces seemed to fit together even though (or perhaps because) edges were left rough and the table had a definite tilt! As a whole, the completed clay work was strongly expressive, allowing Jessica's feelings about as well as her concepts of the kitchen table and its dishes to show.

Jessica made many of her clay pieces with a part-to-whole approach, depending upon subject matter as well as her own inclinations and experience. She broke the clay into pieces and proceeded

125

to add bits together to form objects. This approach is used by many children, especially if they have not had opportunities to observe other ways to work with the clay. In contrast, Myron, from the beginning sessions of clay, seemed to have an understanding of how to make objects from the clay by working from a large mass and pulling out shapes. His objects tended to look more sculptural in that they seemed more formed from a whole and thus integrated. When making a dog, for example, Myron first shaped all of his clay into a roughly formed rectangle with rounded edges. Then he pulled and pinched a head, next legs, and finally a tail. This whole-to-part approach also had the advantage of avoiding the necessity of joining pieces and making them fit. At times Myron's pieces seemed to lack some of the details of the usually smaller and more complex objects made with the part-to-whole method. However, the gain in a stronger, more rounded and three-dimensional form balanced out this lack, and with encouragement and instruction from the teacher, Myron began to explore additional ways to add more textural interest to his work. It is helpful for children to know and experience several approaches to clay construction; they will learn through experience when one method might be more appropriate than another.

Given the time and experience, teachers discover that children can develop unique approaches to expression through clay. Whereas one child sees the dog lying on his bed, another child concentrates on making the dog stand upright; for the first child, the dog is a friendly part of the family; for the other, the dog is on guard and able to attack. Both find ways to show their interpretations in the flexible clay medium so that the result is unique to each child's feelings and concepts. Whether children seek to express an entire world they create or are more in tune with one object made with care and deliberation, clay offers a range of possibilities.

An additional benefit in terms of creating in clay comes from the tolerance clay allows for "mistakes", and for these mistakes to become valued and exciting parts of the work. Once children discover the "game" of trying to find ways to make use of the problems which arise in creating pieces from clay, they are on their way to making use of a creative ability which could be transferred into other areas as well. Learning to utilize the unexpected instead of crying about it allows for the kind of flexibility of thinking to develop which is very helpful in all aspects of living, from solving math problems to putting together a meal from an assorted batch of leftovers! Thus, when Charles discovered his dog's head insisted on bending over, he made a bowl, slid it under the head and announced, "My dog was thirsty!" When Marie saw her bird needed some kind of support to keep it from rolling over, she added a fat worm coming from the bird's beak to the ground, which was a flat piece of clay placed under the bird. When Peter saw that his fingernails had made a pattern on the clay bird he was making, he decided these were feathers and made them all over the bird. Janey saw her bowl getting flatter and flatter; instead of giving in to her tears of frustration, she flattened the clay into a saucer, made a new bowl shape, added a handle, and proudly showed the teacher finished cup and saucer. Because of the flexibility of the medium itself, clay almost encourages children, as they move through a program of clay activities, to experiment, to dare to be different, and to explore the boundaries of their own artistic skills and creativity.

Summary

Using clay in the classroom setting in an ongoing program can help develop skills relating to perceptual/motor, psychological, cognitive, and artistic/creative domains. For some children, clay can be one medium which helps unlock doors which otherwise might remain closed. The child who needs activities to improve hand/eye coordination; the child who has had few opportunities to develop self-confidence; the child who would benefit from a medium which offers cognitive skill-building through a non-threatening, nonverbal three-dimensional material; the child who has the potential to be creative but has never been given the time and the setting to discover that potential: all these children need clay in the classroom.

In Chapter Six, specific information about managing clay in the classroom will be discussed. In addition, the importance of planning clay lessons that will meet both the needs and the interests of children is explained, and three sample clay lessons are provided.

6

CLAY IN YOUR CLASSROOM

Is it possible to have 20 or 30 lively children all engaged in a classroom project using clay without total chaos and without the custodian putting a teacher on a permanent black list? Fortunately, the answer is yes! One of the secrets to avoiding the possible problems which could arise is the secret to many other successful school activities: organization. In the case of clay, management is an overall term which might include a variety of strategies teachers can use with clay specifically regarding preparation, distribution, collection, storage, and, in some cases, finishing. Because how clay is managed is so important for the success of any clay lesson, the first part of this chapter will provide details concerning each of the components. Although for purposes of using clay as a medium for learning, finishing clay pieces is not important, there are occasions when teachers and students may wish to allow certain works to dry and be fired. Therefore, a brief discussion of some of the ways to finish clay pieces is included.

As the saying goes, "Nothing beats experience!" This is applicable to teaching with clay, especially because it may take several lessons using clay with children before individual teachers feel comfortable and in control of the situation. With any new approach or material, teachers inevitably feel somewhat shaky the first time or two. With each experience, confidence can grow, but only if there is adequate preparation, realistic expectations, and a well-thought out plan for operation. Teachers must disregard the stigma often attached to clay in the classroom regarding its manageability. Being willing to go beyond the misinformation, often based upon experiences of teachers who tried clay once and who were not prepared to control the situation, is the first step which must be taken. Using the information found in the following pages may help teachers discover that clay not only offers children opportunities for affective and cognitive learning, but is a medium which can be effectively controlled within the classroom setting.

Acquiring the Proper Clay

While at first it may seem less of a problem to purchase man-made types of modeling materials, there are several reasons why these are not suitable for the kinds of learning experiences described in this book. Oil-based modeling materials, such as Plasticine, usually are sold in a stick form and boxed in a similar fashion to butter or margarine. These materials are responsive to temperature changes; they become hard when cold, and soft when warm. When children are given oil-based materials to use, they must work it between their hands for a time to soften it enough so it can be shaped. The chemical makeup means that this material has a stickiness when warm, which does help make parts stick together at first. However, as objects cool and firm, pieces may begin to separate; if the temperature remains warm, upright sections will droop and eventually fall. Oil-based modeling materials leave an oily residue on hands, tables and clothing which is difficult to remove with water. Dry paper towels are needed to rub surfaces free of the oil before they are washed. Generally, this type of material allows for small, detailed work to be done, but is poorly suited to larger, more sculptural objects. The oil-based material is not very flexible and lacks the degree of responsiveness and forming capacity of earth clays.

When compared to earth clay on a per pound basis, the oil-based materials are more costly. Some natural clays cost as little as 20¢ per pound, whereas a typical oil-based material is $1.75 per pound. Oil-based material should be stored away from extreme temperatures, and since dirt and dust is easily picked up, should be in a closed container. Manufacturers usually offer these modeling mediums in several colors. If several colors are blended, a greyish-brown can result, although some colors do create interesting effects together. Since this is not a permanent type of material, objects made with it should not be displayed for long periods of time, and it is often difficult to transport completed projects if they have projecting or delicate parts.

Doughlike materials (Playdoh is a commercial brand) can be made with ingredients such as flour or salt and cornstarch. All dough type materials share some characteristics in common: they are highly resilient, spongy, and become hard and dry when exposed to air. While lending themselves to more amorphous kinds of objects, such as foods, doughlike materials are difficult to detail and give definite shape. This is why a cookie cutter type of tool is often needed in order to force the medium into a more defined form. Otherwise, products tend to look very similar, no matter what the subject. Connecting parts together can be frustrating, especially for little hands, because the sponginess of the material makes smoothing the parts together hard to do. Children enjoy the kneading and pounding possible with this type of material; its resiliency especially seems to make these activities satisfying. Dough type materials don't lend themselves to large, sculptural forms. Once children are ready to express themselves in more definite and expressive ways, doughlike mediums can become more frustrating than helpful.

Doughlike materials need to be kept tightly wrapped or they will dry out; once dried, they cannot be moistened and reused. Refrigeration will help retard mold on the homemade varieties. Products made from these substances can be air-dried and then baked in an ordinary oven to make them more permanent. They can then be painted and shellacked. Compared to earth clays, dough types, when commercially made, are more expensive on a pound-per-pound basis. However, the homemade varieties can be quite inexpensive.

Earth clays are handled by many companies which supply art materials to schools. Most cities have at least one firm which specializes in clay, and which may mix their own clay bodies. Anyone who has traveled across parts of the United States no doubt realizes that there are many earth colors, ranging from the palest beige to the deepest brown, or from the lightest red to an intense rust. These are the same colors which can be found in clays. After being dug from the ground, clay is processed by removing grit and stones; it can be put into a powdered form for easy shipment to various parts of the country. Clay is sold either in a powdered form, with several types blended together, or in moist condition. Usually commercial dealers distribute the clay in 25 pound bags, whether powdered or moist; often the moist clay comes in two 25 pound bags per box. If a school plans to buy clay, and there is no system-wide buying procedure, it would be wise to attempt to get bids from several companies. Costs

132

of shipping must be considered if distance is involved, which is why a local dealer may be better even if prices are somewhat higher. If finances are a problem, the dry clay is significantly cheaper. However, moist clay is much easier in terms of time and readiness for use.

Generally, earth clays are divided into the white and red classification. Red clays are particularly appropriate for pottery and for work which requires a flexible, highly responsive medium. Artists may use red clay to make sketches of ideas for possible sculptures. Children seem to enjoy the color of the red clay, which dries to a light color and deepens if it is fired. It is easy to manipulate and responds well to kneading and pounding. White clays are denser than the red clays, and therefore are particularly appropriate for sculptural forms. It provides a firmer support to upright or more detailed work, and takes somewhat longer to dry. White clay looks grey or bluish when wet, and does not turn completely white unless it is dried and then fired. Many artists like white clay under some glazes because the colors seem brighter. For classroom use by young children, either type of clay is satisfactory. Red clay is generally more flexible in its usage, so if available at the same or less cost as the white it would be the best purchase.

Preparing the Clay

For the remainder of the discussion about the preparation, distribution, collection, storage and finishing of clay, earth clay will be meant when the word clay is used. In preparation of clay, the proper amount of moisture must be maintained or children will become frustrated. If the clay is too wet, it will stick to working surfaces and to the hands; if it is too dry, it crumbles and cannot be formed. To determine the right amount of moisture, teachers need to test the clay on a regular basis by picking up a piece and handling it. When moist clay is purchased, bags should be checked immediately to be certain the clay is of the right consistency (a good test is to open the bag and see if a finger can be pushed into the clay easily). Even a small puncture in the bag which holds clay can eventually cause dryness.

Clay which is purchased in dry form can be mixed in any amount needed. Several procedures can be used; one is to place the dry clay in a large, easy to clean container, then add water in cupfuls, mixing after each addition. When the consistency allows the clay to be balled up without excessive sticking to hands, it can be allowed to sit for a day or so to "cure." This allows the particles of clay to absorb all the moisture, and creates the flexibility needed for good clay. Clay which is curing can be wrapped loosely if it is fairly moist and if it will be unused only for a day or two.

A 25 pound bag of moist clay will provide a class of 25 children each with a ball of clay about the size of an orange; this is sufficient for most projects attempted by young children. The size of a child's hands should help determine the amount of clay to be provided when doing pinch pots or pieces which require shaping with the hands. Children will discover it is frustrating and difficult to control a ball of clay which is too large to fit comfortably in their two hands.

If clay which was moist has gotten semi-hard and is too firm to cut easily with string or fishing line, it needs to be reconditioned. There is professional ceramic equipment available which reprocesses clay, but this may not be available in some school systems or may be difficult to utilize. One way to recondition clay in the classroom is to try to cut it or break it into as many small pieces as possible. These should be placed in a plastic container with a lid which fits tightly. Moist toweling should be put between layers of clay. Old terrycloth towels work well, or other types of heavy material; strong paper towels will work for short periods of time since they tend to disintegrate after a time. If the clay needs only a little moistening, one wet towel on top and several hours in the airtight container might be enough. However, the best approach is to leave the clay overnight and check the next morning to see if more water is needed. Too much water can also be a problem, and the container might need draining if water has accumulated on the bottom. It helps to turn the entire container upside down after a period of time, since this is likely to distribute the moisture more evenly.

Distributing the Clay

One of the most exciting ways to first introduce clay to a class or group of children is to place an unopened bag of moist clay on a table so it can be seen by everyone. (The bag should be stood upright, pounding the bottom a few times against the table will flatten it to prevent wobbling.) Starting at the top, the bag should be peeled away and removed. Then, with a piece of heavy thread, thin string, or best of all, nylon finishing line, (a washer or heavy wooden bead can be tied to either end of a piece about 18" long for a better grip), the clay is cut by slowly pulling the line down the center of the clay. After several vertical cuts, the clay can then be sliced horizontally in thicknesses of about one to two inches. Pieces of the clay can be removed so that each child will receive a slice which is approximately one by four inches. Children can roll these into balls, or begin immediately flattening them, etc., depending upon the particular lesson.

For most projects made by young children, wedging, which is the process of removing air bubbles from the clay by slamming pieces onto a flat surface, is not necessary. Children should know about this process, and why it is necessary. Pieces which will be fired need to be made with wedged clay because air bubbles which are trapped inside the clay can expand under the heat of the kiln and explode, causing the object to disintegrate. Since most clay objects made in an ongoing clay program will not be saved for later firing, the wedging process need not be part of the lesson; however, if pieces will be saved, it is wise to have clay wedging occur, with each child spending a few minutes throwing the clay down hard on the table or on burlap or kraft paper placed on the floor. Because commercially processed clay has gone through a cleaning and conditioning treatment, clay bought in a moist state needs little additional preparation for products which are small and contain few thick, solid sections.

Before any clay is put before any child, several important steps should be taken. These steps, which quickly become part of a regular routine and need only a few minutes of time, will make the working and cleanup periods much easier and more pleasant for both children and the teacher! Smocks or a short-sleeved man's shirt buttoned on

135

backwards can be worn by those children who might need extra protection for light-colored or dressier types of clothing. Most teachers discover that few children require any type of covering once the control of the clay medium has been established and understood. A piece of burlap about 12 by 18 inches or a heavy-duty type of large grocery bag can be placed before each child. The burlap, which is inexpensive and easy to find in fabric stores, is preferable; in addition to defining the child's work area, it will keep the table from sticking to the clay; create an instant texture for at least one side of the clay as it is shaped; and make cleanup easier. The burlap can be reused over many months; the paper sacks will begin to disintegrate after several sessions with clay. The burlap can be shaken clean after each clay lesson (any clay which clings to the material will shake off after it dries), and pieces can easily be stacked and stored.

Each child should be given two wet paper towels (foam meat trays from the grocery store make excellent holders for the towels and are easy to stack and carry from table to table). One towel is to be used for moistening hands while working with the clay; clay surfaces will begin to dry out as the lesson progresses, and small amounts of moisture on hands will make the shaping easier. The second towel is used during cleanup time to clean clay from hands. *Under no circumstances should water be placed on tables where children will be working with the clay*! This is one major reason why so many teachers decide that clay is too messy to use in the classroom. When clay is allowed to become too wet, it liquifies and becomes impossible to control. Liquid clay is, in fact, important in the process of creating with clay. Called slip, liquid clay is used to coat surfaces of those pieces of clay which will be joined together, and is usually brushed on after the surface has been scored (roughened) so that adhesion is maximized and parts will stay together even after drying. Slip is also used by potters and ceramatists to pour into molds such as those designed for dishware. However, slip is not appropriate for forming handmade types of sculpture and ceramics! Once teachers, and students, discover the ease and sufficiency of the wet towel method, clay lessons almost magically become easier to control during the time pieces are being made and during the cleanup period. Towels can be distributed by a child who is given a plastic pail with a small

136

amount of water at the bottom. The paper towels (the prefolded variety work best) are placed in the water and then can be taken out one at a time, squeezed of excess water if needed, and placed on the side of each working area.

Covering the entire table where a group of children will be working with clay is not necessary; most tables found in preschool and primary classrooms, for example, have easy-to-clean surfaces and any clay which might stray from the individual areas is easily wiped off with a sponge or towels. However, if burlap is not available and if the paper bag idea is not possible for some reason, large pieces of the kraft paper which comes on a roll, and which is found in most school supply rooms, can be cut to fit each table. Unless the clay is unusually wet, the sheets can be saved and reused several times. Newspaper, either for individual work areas or for covering the tables, should be avoided; this type of paper is thin and absorbs moisture rapidly. Not only will newspaper quickly fall apart and become caught in clay pieces, it also may cause clay to dry out. In fact, if wetness is a problem, newspapers *can* be used to absorb some of the excess moisture before clay is given to the children to use.

Facilitating the Clay Experience

The basic tools for anyone working in clay are the hands, and should be the primary emphasis in teaching young children about the processes of shaping and forming. However, there may be more advanced children, particular types of lessons, or particular needs which seem to indicate the use of some additional tools might be helpful. Clay tools do not need to be expensive; those made for professionals can quickly run into hundreds of dollars. Instead, children can be encouraged to create their own tools. Popsickle sticks, broken lengthwise, make excellent cutting tools; old kitchen utensils, combs, stirring sticks, bobby pins, toothpicks, small dowel rods, all can be used for a variety of purposes. Avoid pencils; many children use these to poke holes which turn out to be identical in size and often add little or nothing to the appearance of the piece.

Holes for eyes should be discussed with children, since an awareness of the eye fitting into the socket can result in more expressive figures. Children should be able to understand that pencils are a drawing tool, and not appropriate for clay. Of course, there may be times when incising (cutting) lines into a particular clay piece, such as the addition of a border design into the sides of a vase, might be valid, but until children understand the differences between drawing and poking with pencils on clay, it would be wise to utilize other types of tools with the clay.

Most young children ignore clay tools unless a particular need arises. Even if shown how to use tools by the teacher, many children at the preschool and primary levels will try them out, but quickly return to their hands as the shaping force. This is an indication that children are not ready for tools, and attempting to interest them in using tools would be detrimental rather then beneficial. Teachers may realize, however, as clay lessons progress, that some instruction about clay tools could result in those children who are ready being prepared to utilize some kinds of devices which would assist them in shaping or texturing their pieces. Having some tools available in a central location once instruction has been given would allow those who feel the need for tools to make use of them.

During the time that children are creating their clay works, there should be few, if any, management needs. If children have clay which is in good condition, a well-defined work space, an understanding of the expected behavior, and experience in such techniques as keeping hands moist, the work period should find each child intent on the creative act of making objects with clay. Of course, teachers should be on the alert for problems such as clay drying out too fast (sometimes having a child trade in a lump of clay which is too dry for another more moist one is less of a problem than struggling to condition the clay during a work period). Hopefully, because it is during the working time that teachers need to be utilizing the teaching strategies which will enable children to develop both cognitively and affectively, little time will need to be spent on the mechanics of using clay. Having time to work with individual as well as groups of children should become more of a reality after the first two or three clay lessons when children become accustomed to the routine and the responsibilities.

Because all children will not complete their clay activities within the same time period, teachers need to be aware of which children might be finishing early. In some cases, such children might need to be helped to slow down and improve their skills at joining pieces, adding textures, etc. Other children might be able to assist in some management need which could be met while other children are still working. An example might be wetting the towels which will be used between layers of clay in the container or being certain that the sponges used for cleaning are prepared. At times, some children might benefit from an additional project made of clay which could be related to the completed topic or idea: A birdhouse to go with the bird; a family of people who own the dog; a table to go under the bowls. Just as in the area of reading some children finish long before others and need direction about additional activities, so some children will complete clay projects before others. If teachers are prepared for this event and children discover there is flexibility regarding how the clay period is structured, both will have a more positive and beneficial experience.

Collecting and Storing Clay

At the conclusion of the clay lesson, all children should assist in the cleanup process. Each child should roll clay back into a ball and then put it into the designated container. A small plastic garbage can, or a large diaper bucket, also plastic, work well as containers for clay if they have lids which will fit tightly. If only a metal container is available, it should first be lined with a heavy plastic bag. To make certain that clay will receive enough moisture to prepare it for the next clay lesson, have the children slightly flatten each ball before it is placed in the container. This allows more of the clay surface to come into contact with moisture. After each layer of clay, several damp towels should be placed on top. Don't use burlap since it is a loosely woven material which easily could fall apart and get caught in clay; it also has a strong odor when wet. Layers of towels do not need to be dripping wet unless the clay has become particularly dry. At the top of the container, after adding the last layer of towels, additional water can be added by pouring small amounts into the top towels. This is particularly recommended if there will be a number of days between clay lessons. Lids must fit tightly; even a small amount of air will create hardness in clay after a time. If a lid doesn't seem airtight, a plastic bag which will fit inside the container can be used and tied tightly around the clay. The container should be checked periodically to see if moisture is adequate; usually if the top layer of toweling is dry, more moisture is needed and there might be leakage somewhere. An airtight container should be able to keep clay in workable condition for extended lengths of time. Turning clay upside down inside the container, or when possible, turning the entire container upside down, helps distribute any water which might collect at the bottom.

If clay is allowed to sit inside a container for some length of time, mold can develop. This is not harmful, and can usually be scraped off the surface of the clay with any sharp edge (ruler, knife, etc.). Since clay comes from the earth, children should understand why mold might form; a related science lesson could make use of some of the questions children might have about the mold.

Amazingly enough, one paper towel is usually sufficient for cleaning hands. Unless clay was unusually wet during the lesson, the small amount of clay left on hands wipes off easily with the towel. If a more extensive handwashing is indicated, don't use a sink which has no trap. Clay will, after time, accumulate and clog the pipes. Instead, use a bucket which contains a small amount of water; the bucket should be placed on the floor with several layers of newspapers underneath and paper towels nearby. Once the routine is established, only a few minutes should be needed for cleanup. Jobs can be assigned on an alternating basis for such tasks as collecting burlap or paper, throwing away the two towels, wiping off tables, etc. It is important children realize that the cleanup process is important to the total lesson, and that the professional sculptor or potter takes excellent care of all his or her supplies and materials as well.

Clay which finds its way onto floors can be swept up once it has dried; large pieces should be picked up immediately after the lesson is completed to avoid being stepped upon. Those rooms with carpeting can be cleaned with the vacuum sweeper by the custodian at the usual time, and should present no problems. If children are shown ways to keep clay away from edges of the table, and to keep small crumbs of clay picked up by pressing them into a moist ball held in the hand, little clay will fall on the floor.

Custodians are important people, and should be told ahead of time when clay is to be used on a regular basis, and why. Perhaps if custodians understand the importance of using clay, and that after a short time it will be less and less likely to create for them any additional cleanup, they will be less likely to shudder when they discover a teacher is using clay in the classroom. The importance of helping children learn is, of course, the overall concern of all members of school staffs. If clay is an additional medium which has a unique and vital contribution to make to that learning process, then it should be supported by administrators, teachers and custodians. Children, when they regard the clay sessions as important and special, will be willing to help in any way possible to manage the clay experience so it can be repeated over and over.

Finishing Selected Clay Pieces

Many teachers find it difficult to believe that young children willingly return clay to the container after each lesson, not fussing about keeping their efforts for that day. Once children understand that clay is to be offered to them on a regular basis, and that clay is not necessarily a material which has to be turned into a final product worthy of being "saved" each time it is used, they readily accept the balling up of clay pieces. There simply isn't a need to cling to the objects which might result from any one experience, because the children understand the experience can be repeated. As has been mentioned earlier in the book, it is the process which really means the most to young children; it is often the adults who regard the products as "cute" or "clever" and worthy of preservation! Certainly children need to be aware of how artists use clay for sketching and exploring ideas, not expecting these to become the finished pieces. This directly parallels what can work well for children as well: regarding clay as a learning medium which helps in the exploration and discovery of ideas. To contrast a room of children who have been using clay for several months in this manner with another class which has grudgingly been allowed to have one clay experience for that year bears out the differences. While the first group of children is relaxed, confident and explorative, the second is tense, worried and awkward. For one group, clay is a familiar medium which lends itself to the extension of the learning experience in many directions; for the other, clay is unfamiliar and perhaps frustrating, with little opportunity for discovery.

Despite the use of clay for the learning experience, there will be times when teachers and students may wish to preserve clay products. This seems particularly appropriate after children have had enough time to develop skills, and products reflect the control and understanding of the medium gained during that time period. It may not be necessary to tell a group of children that pieces will be saved on a particular day, although this is certainly possible. If additional time is needed to be sure certain joints are smoothed together well and a more finished look achieved, teachers may decide to announce when products will be kept for drying and then firing. If pieces are to be saved, they should each be marked on the bottom with the child's initials and date; if several classes will be firing pieces at the same time, it is wise to additionally mark each piece with a code for the particular class (teacher's initials usually work well). Children may find it difficult to recognize a clay piece after several weeks and after it has gone through the firing process, so identifications are important and should be put on works as they are completed and still soft. Professional sculptors and potters often design a mark to place on their works, and this mark plus a certain date may make some pieces more valuable than others once an artist becomes well-known. Discovering that artists sign and date pieces may help children become aware of this process as more than just a way to find their own pieces again! Asking a professional sculptor or potter to visit the school could be a stimulating way to introduce young children to ways in which adults engage in art for careers as well as for self-expression. Even better, of course, would be taking a group of children to visit an artist in the studio where pots are thrown or clay shaped into works of sculpture.

Clay pieces which are to be fired need to be put somewhere where they will not be handled or bumped while drying (about a week). Pieces should be on a flat surface, and not stacked, so that bottoms can dry flat. Don't use cardboard under drying pieces since it will absorb the moisture from the clay and warp, creating an uneven surface under the clay. Turning objects occasionally during the drying time helps avoid cracking; if one part of the clay remains wet while others dry, separation can occur. Slowly drying clay pieces is also less likely to result in cracks. Clay products which have not been fired are called greenware. Greenware has the most potential for breakage since it is brittle and easily damaged. Children should be prepared for possible damage, especially if pieces have delicate or protruding parts.

Many schools have kilns, which are the special ovens designed for firing clay. Children should be taught the correct terms (kiln not oven; fire not bake) as part of their vocabulary. Kilns should be operated by persons familiar with the necessary procedures; usually several teachers in each school have an understanding of the kiln and should be willing to teach others or do the firing. Each kiln can have its own characteristics, but most have similar parts. Newer kilns may have an automatic shut-off switch so that when the proper internal temperature is reached, the kiln will turn itself off. Instructions provided by the company who either manufactures or sells the kiln should be carefully followed. Kilns should never be left unattended when at higher temperatures, and should be in locations away from children and with adequate provisions for the amount of heat generated (venting may be needed for large kilns). Clay products which have not completely dried may explode in the kiln. One way to test pieces for dryness is to hold a piece up to the cheek; those with some moisture feel cold rather than cool. Try comparing a piece which has been drying for at least a week with one which has only been completed recently to check out this difference. Greenware pieces can be loaded into the kiln so that they touch each other; if arranged carefully, products can be nested to save space. Most kilns have several shelves which can be arranged at a variety of heights to allow for clay pieces of varying sizes.

Once the clay has been fired, which takes a full 24 hours since the kiln must be given time both to heat up and to cool down, pieces are called bisqueware. Many children's clay products look better if left in the natural bisqueware state, particularly if the objects are sculptural in design. Pottery pieces may be painted using a variety of materials. The traditional finish for clay is called glaze; glazes are made with many of the same minerals found in glass and provide a glass-like coating to the surface of the clay which can make it waterproof. Glossy (shiny), semi-glossy, or matt (dull) are three types of finishes found in glazes. Colors range from one end of the spectrum to the other, although certain colors cost much more than others due to the more expensive ingredients needed. Reds are expensive and are also sometimes difficult to fire without losing the color. A glaze chart is needed for selecting colors since some glazes before firing look to be a completely different color than they will be after the minerals have been affected by the extreme temperatures of the kiln.

Glaze should not be applied to the bottom of clay pieces as this will cause them to stick to the support that is used to hold them during the firing, and may also drip off the pieces onto the shelf in the kiln. Since glazes act like molten glass when at high temperatures, allowing pieces to touch each other or parts of the kiln during firing will mean that, as the objects cool, they will adhere to those surfaces which are touched. Directions on applying glazes usually come with the commercially prepared types of glaze, and should be followed for best results. Greenware and glazed pieces should not be fired together, since if a greenware piece would explode, bits of clay could become imbedded in the glazed surfaces, ruining many if not all of the pieces.

Temperatures for both the greenware and the glaze firings can be determined by the type of clay being used and by the directions given by the companies manufacturing and/or distributing the clays or glazes. Cones are triangles of clay which have been prepared to bend or "melt" at certain temperatures within the kiln. They are numbered according to their range of temperature sensitivity. A cone is placed in a lump of soft clay and placed on a shelf within the kiln in front of a peephole made for that purpose in the side of the kiln. When the kiln is at the highest temperatures (most kilns have low, medium and high switches which are activated at intervals until the kiln is at the highest temperature), the cone should be checked periodically to see when the desired temperature has been reached; then the kiln is shut off manually or, if there is a kiln sitter or automatic shut-off, power is cut off by the cone when it bends.

Because glazing is a complex process which requires additional time and places much emphasis on the finishing of the products, teachers may decide that pottery pieces can be painted or colored with less complicated materials. Tempera or watercolor paints will provide colorful finishes to clay which has been fired; since these media will rub off clay pieces, a coat of shellac can be applied. Brushing shellac over water-based paints can cause them to run together, so spray shellac is best. Spray shellac should be applied where ventilation is adequate; teachers may prefer to do this part of the process themselves, since shellac is difficult to remove from hands and other surfaces! Acrylic types of paint also work well on clay, and since they need no shellacking, may be less of a problem than waterbased paints. An acrylic gloss or matt medium can be applied over the acrylic paints to add luster to finished pieces.

Another way to finish clay pieces, especially those with more flat areas, is shoe polish. The waxiness of the polish provides a shine after the color has been applied and then buffed. The shoe polish finish can look particularly good on objects which need just a little additional color to improve the finished appearance. Only a little polish is required, so this can be an economical way to complete a project.

Sample Clay Lessons for the Classroom

Earlier chapters have discussed the various subjects which were used in the clay research study. From data gathered about children from ages four to eight, as well as from the various workshops and classroom visitations since the research was completed, certain topics which seem to particularly interest children can be determined. When these are matched with the characteristics of the clay medium so that subjects are appropriate for clay and vice versa, planning for clay lessons can be done with the expectation of helping children develop cognitive and affective skills to the fullest extent possible.

To fully utilize the potential of any subject used during the clay lessons, as rich and as meaningful a preparation time as possible should be planned. Children who have a thorough understanding of birds, at the level to which it is possible for their particular age group and ability level, will bring to the making of clay birds much more interest and awareness of possibilities than children who have had no preparation. Of course, the enthusiasm of the teacher, the type of setting, the kinds of aids utilized, all have impact upon the outcome of a lesson. Not all teachers and not all children have the same interests; some lessons will appeal more to some children and some teachers than to others. However, when clay lessons are presented in an ongoing manner, with activities arranged so that concepts are linked and skills build upon each other, each lesson assumes importance in the total program of learning through clay. Lessons must be centered around the experiences, activities and interests of the particular group being taught. An awareness also must be developed in regards to individual children's needs, interests and skill levels. A well-designed clay lesson should be flexible enough to allow for low, medium and high levels of skills regarding both the cognitive and the artistic aspects.

Providing time for children to work on ideas of their own is essential to the full integration of those concepts which have been introduced by the teacher. Only by allowing time for ideas to become part of each child's thinking process, and to be reinterpreted by the child in individual ways, do those ideas truly become "owned" by each child. Children need time to assimilate what has been

146

presented or experienced, and clay works well with this need since it is forgiving of mistakes, adaptable to a wide range of skill levels, and flexible and manipulative enough to allow for the expression of many ideas in a three-dimensional interpretation. It may surprise teachers to discover that children use the "free time" periods of clay exploration to experiment and even return to earlier, possibly more basic, skill levels. This is, in fact, evidence of the assimilation process occurring as the child goes back to pick up what might have been hazy or not quite completed on the first time through. Or it could indicate that a particular child was not ready for a concept and needs the time to return and work through a particular idea. It may also surprise some that a high level of creativity can emerge from the more structured lessons, especially when time and support are given for this creativity to reveal itself. This phenomenon is true in other areas as well; in mathematics, for example, some of the greatest, most creative advances occurred after years of intensive, highly structured investigation and study. The mind must be prepared to be creative.

It may seem a long way from the explorations of young children to the discoveries of reknown scientists and mathematicians. But, in the beginnings are found the seeds of what may happen in the future. Even the young child can discover the joy of creativity and recognize that having the right tools — including ideas — is vital to the discovery process. Teachers can assist in many direct and indirect ways so that children have the time, the place, the materials, and the ideas, which, when combined in unique ways by each child, can facilitate the creative process. The kind of creativity being suggested here is not only tied to the artistic expression possible, but to the way in which ideas or concepts are interpreted or connected together. When lessons are presented in ways that allow children to see the links between various concepts, even though these may seem simple and basic to adults, leaps can be made in terms of learning. The idea that the bird's nest is in many ways similar to the pinchpot; that the shape of the bird's body is almost identical to the egg which the birds lays; that the bird's wings allow it to make a nest in a tree, and that the nest is rounded to fit between branches so it won't fall;

147

all ideas which to an adult seem ordinary, but to a child discovering the connections, exciting and new.

Three lessons, all linked, are included in the remainder of this chapter. They serve to illustrate the kinds of subjects young children enjoy; the ways in which teachers might attempt to adapt strategies to fit the skills of various children; and a variety of suggestions about vocabulary, visual aids, and techniques, to be used with the clay. It is hoped that teachers will discover, through their own interests as well as those of the particular students they teach, other subjects, and that these will become part of an ongoing program which helps children learn through the medium of clay.

Lesson One
Bowls

Pottery Lesson

Readiness: Set a mood earlier in the day
that will start children thinking about
pots or other kinds of containers.

— why do we need them?
— who makes them?
— what are they made of?
— what can we call them?
    (dishes, bowls, pots, etc.)

Gather together a collection of bowls of
many sizes and made of different materials. Have several made of clay. Read the
story *Goldilock and the Three Bears* (better yet have the children tell you the
story!) Ask the children to explain what
bowls the bears used and why they were
each different and how they were similar.
Ask them to choose from your collection
of bowls the one they believe Papa Bear
would have liked, then Mama Bear, and,
finally, Baby Bear. Have a discussion of
sizes, shapes, tops, bottoms, insides, and
outsides of bowls. Ask questions such as:

149

Why does a bowl need sides?
Why does a bowl need an opening?
Why does a bowl need a bottom?
Does the bottom need to be flat?

Demonstration:

How to make a pinchpot bowl:

Practice how to make a pinchpot from a ball of clay. Ask an art teacher to work with you if this would be helpful. Follow the step-by-step drawing to try the method. Demonstrate the technique to the class.

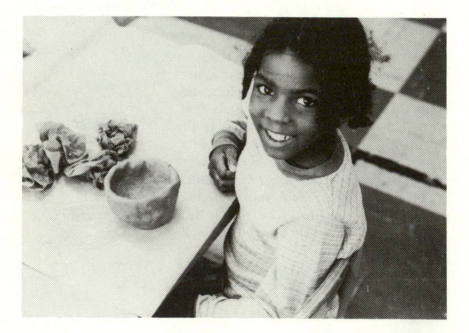

Making a clay bowl, pinch pot method

1. Start with a ball of clay big enough to fit in between hands comfortably. (Grapefruit size for adults, orange size for small hands!).

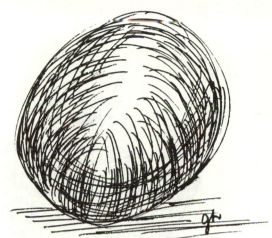

2. After the clay is rounded, put a thumbprint where you want to start the opening of the pot . . .

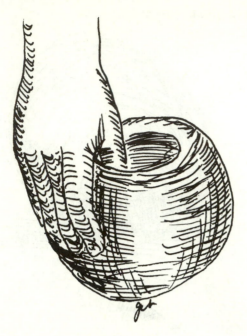

3. Begin to open pot by using thumb on the inside of the top opening. Put fingers on the outside. Press thumb towards fingers, squeezing clay in between. Turn pot slowly, and pinch as you turn. Overlap each pinch.

4.
When the opening is large enough, use both thumbs on the inside and all fingers on the outside. Continue to pinch slowly so bowl will have sides of equal thickness.

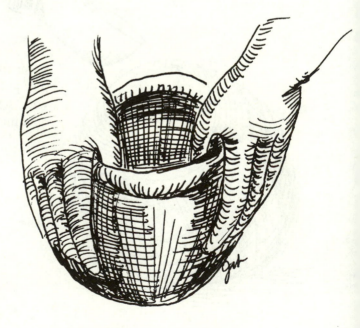

* Remember: you can moisten hands and then smooth the clay, but *don't* put water directly on clay!

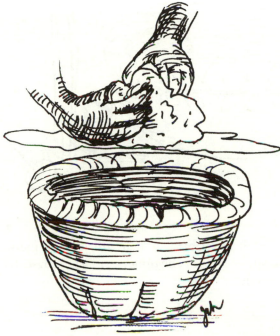

5. Some cracks normally appear on the rim or edges. Small amounts of wet clay or smoothing with moistened hands will quickly even out the cracks unless the clay was too dry to use. Don't try to make pinch pots with stiff or crumbly clay!

6. Coils can be added to make the bowl higher or create a variety of shapes. Each coil must be moist and even. Cut exactly the length needed — don't overlap ends or bowl will become lopsided.

7. Texture may be added with any object which will make a mark. Repeat designs are usually best for beginners. Flatten base by pressing bowl gently on table.

8. Don't hesitate to roll your pot back into a ball, moisten and be ready to start again another time.

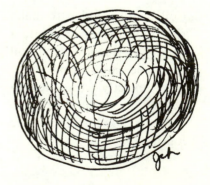

Activity Time

Children move to work areas, clay is given out or is already on tables. Wet paper towels are used to moisten hands and clay during work with clay. (A clay management lesson should have been taught before the first clay lesson). Have children form a pinchpot with you. Go very slowly. Ask children to squeeze their first try back into a ball and try to form a pinchpot without you doing one with them. Observe carefully which children may need extra help and encouragement. Move around so each child can get a comment on his or her work. Question and support individual children according to the individual level at which they are presently working:

> Higher Level: How can you put texture on your bowl?
> How can you put designs on it?
> How can you change the shape?

> Average Level: How can you change the shape?

> Lower Level: Can you roll the clay into a ball?
> Show me how to pinch the clay.

Followup

At either this session or the next (each lesson should be repeated at least once), have the children group the bowls together in the center of a table and discover:

> Which bear would like which bowl?
> Which bowls are the tallest?
> Which bowls have the widest opening?
> Etc.

Additional Suggestions

Social Studies correlation: How bowls have been used to study past civilizations. Sometimes fragments of bowls are all that tell us dates of certain cultures. On our own continent, a study of Indians and how they made bowls and their importance to various tribes could involve history, culture and symbolism. Going from a bowl used by one of your students for morning cereal to another bowl used by an Indian 200 years ago to eat his cereal (maize?) might present a child with a meaningful learning experience, especially when he discovers he can make a bowl much like the clay bowl used by an Indian child.

Art Appreciation: Ask an art teacher or local artist to visit the class and explain how professional potters work. If possible, visit an art room or studio where someone can demonstrate throwing a pot on a wheel. Explain the difference between handmade and thrown pots or bowls.

Vocabulary Words

potter	pottery
opening	texture
bottom	pinch pot
round	size
bowl	container

Lesson Two
Birds

Making Clay Birds

Readiness: Take a bird watcher's walk around the neighborhood. See who can spot the most birds. Put up a bird feeder outside the window of your classroom or as near to the room as possible. Have the children keep track of kinds of birds that visit. Have large picture books of birds where children can look at them. Put up large pictures of birds. Show a film about birds; play records with bird sounds or songs about birds.

Discussion/Observation: Ask the children to tell you what they know about birds. Using models or photographs of birds, help the children find

similarities	textures
differences	positions
shapes	parts
sizes	

Demonstration:

How to form a bird from an egg! Make an egg-shaped ball of clay. Using the whole-to-part method, pull and pinch the parts of the bird from the ball. (Is there a bird hiding in this egg? Let's see if he'll come out!) Follow the step-by-step drawings before you try making a bird with the class.

157

1. Begin by form-
   ing an oval
   shape or egg
   between your
   hands. Don't
   roll on the
   table or shape
   will flatten!

2.
Pinch and pull
out a head shape
and beak from
the egg. Squeeze
back into egg
shape and try
again if first at-
tempt doesn't
seem right.

158

3. Use fingers or a tool to carve out the shape of a wing on either side of the egg body.   Pull out a piece from the back of the egg to make a tail.

4. Use extra clay if you want to add legs and feet. To balance the bird, you might put it on a rock shape or branch, or fold the legs underneath for a resting position. Add eyes but not with a hole — eyes are not empty sockets!

5. Have fun adding texture for feathers. What could the bird hold in its mouth?

Additional Suggestions

Birds can become the focal point of a beginning science unit. Even a city child should have some knowledge of birds, and learning more about them could be correlated with many activities related to the child's own interests and capabilities. The bird feeder could provide some direct experiences with birds. Local pet stores are often willing to provide visits from their collection, or there may be a bird owner on your staff who would be willing to bring a bird to spend a day.

There are a number of well-illustrated children's books about birds, both fiction and non-fiction. Your school or local librarian should be able to provide you with an extensive collection. Using one of the many records available which have songs about birds, have children enjoy a physical activity time pretending to be birds and flying to the music.

Vocabulary Words

oval	pulling out
egg shape	shaping
texture	flying
shell	size

parts of the bird: body, head, feet, claws, eyes, etc.

Activity Time

Children move to work areas; clay is given out or is already on tables. Have children form an egg-shaped ball with you. Go slowly. (We need to go slowly, children, so the shell won't break!) Once the children have made the egg shape, tell them to begin forming the head by pinching and pulling the clay at one end of the egg. Observe carefully as you move around the room which children may need

162

extra help and encouragement. Question and support individual children according to the level at which they are working:

Higher Level: What does your bird need to cover his skin?
Where is your bird (on the ground, a branch, flying?)
Encourage blending together all parts so they will hold together.

Average Level: Encourage textures, blending and details.

Lower Level: Try to help children understand the egg shape. Redemonstrate, if needed.

Followup

Have the birds "visit" other tables to get acquainted. Guide children into discussing how they made the birds and naming parts; describing what their birds like to eat, do, etc.

Lesson Three
Birds and Nests

Making Birds and Nests

Readiness: Repeat some of the activities and ideas from the bird lesson which seem appropriate or which you think children need. See if you can locate a science film which shows a bird building a nest. Ask children to bring nests from home if they have any. If possible, visit a hatchery to see baby chicks being born, or borrow the equipment and hatch a few eggs in the classroom.

Discussion/Observation: When the children gather to talk about their readiness experiences, try to draw out information and ideas about nests:

shapes of nests
placement of nests
how birds are hatched
what birds eat
how baby birds are fed
parts of birds
etc.

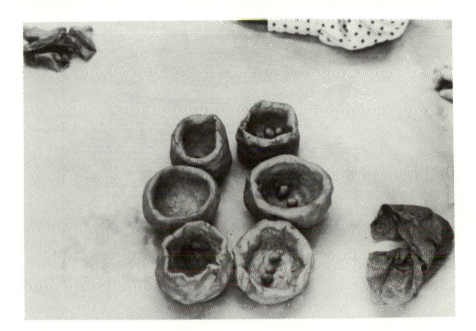

Demonstration:

Ask the children to remind you how to make a pinch pot. Make one, following their directions, and help them remember as you work. Ask the children how the pinch pot reminds them of a nest. How could it be made to look more like a nest? (Textures, eggs, twigs, etc.)

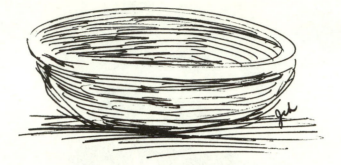

1. Refer back to the directions for making a pinch pot. . . Use this method for starting the clay nest, but open pot at the top so birds and eggs will fit inside.

2. Texture the nest using fingers or tools. Leave it lumpy-looking — it will make the nest look more authentic!

166

3. Add at least one bird, using some of the methods learned during the bird lesson (or experiment and try a new method). Make small eggs to go under the bird — maybe even one that is hatching!

Ask the children to think of other methods they could use to make a nest. Explain that they may choose a way to make a nest and then will make a bird who might like to live in that nest (perhaps with a family!). Help children remember how to make birds.

Activity Time

Children move to work areas; clay is given out or is already on tables. If there are some children still having trouble forming the clay into either a ball or egg, work with them for a time. Encourage children to make a nest first, then birds, eggs, etc. Try to visit each child to offer a word of praise and any needed suggestions. Use the questioning technique to help children see more possibilities.

> Higher Level: What is your nest made from?
> How can you show this with the clay?
> Can you show a baby bird coming out of one of these eggs you made in the nest?
>
> Average Level: Encourage textures and details.
>
> Lower Level: Show me how you can make an egg of clay.
> Where is the bird's head on this egg going to be?
> Etc.

Followup

Take a tour or bird walk around the class to see the variety of nests and birds. Give as many children a chance to talk about their own clay work as possible.

168

Additional Suggestions

A social studies unit on the variety of kinds of homes inhabited by kinds of animals could be an off-shoot of the birds and nests lesson. Building on the two earlier lessons on bowls and birds, children could be helped to see how seemingly unrelated ideas can be connected. For a physical activity, have children find a spot on the playground and using leaves, twigs, etc., build nests large enough to sit in. What could "pretend eggs" be made from?

Vocabulary Words

nest	hatching
home	feeding
caring	family

CLAY IN AN AGE OF TECHNOLOGY

To advocate clay as a medium for learning to an educator of the 80's and 90's might appear to be archaic. In the technological age, surely it must be the computer which holds the answers, not a lump of clay! It is television which holds youth enthralled, not crayons and paint; video games seduce even the younger children while dance and drama are ignored. Do the arts offer enough to compete with such a dazzling array of mechanical devices and sophisticated hardware? Or is this, in fact, a question which should even need to be asked?

Visiting many preschool and primary schools gives credence to the notion that young children today have few opportunities to become aware of the potential of the arts. How much time is spent in the life of a four or five year old on exploring with a medium such as paint? How much time is allowed for experimenting with clay? Are young children still encouraged to engage in dramatic play; to dance and to sing to their own music instead of that heard on the radio or television set? Instead of regarding the arts as an essential part of every child's growing and developing process, educators have begun to race children through a program designed to instill the most knowledge in the least amount of time. At age four, children in some schools are expected to have extensive vocabularies, even if they have no understanding of what the words mean. Emphasis is placed heavily on the cognitive end of the learning process, and balance between the intellectual and the emotional needs is weakened. The Position Paper for the Association for Childhood Education International (1976) delineates the dilemma:

> The earlier and earlier introduction of a subject-matter-skill focus creates dichotomy and discontinuity at the very time that learning should be continuous and integral.

> No one can deny the importance of a literate population — one in which everyone can read, compute and communicate. The introduction of departmentalization of reading, math and language specialists earlier and earlier in schooling and the emphasis on reading and math in kindergarten may seem commonsensible approaches. But this press for basics overlooked the self-organization and the basic responsiveness and rhythm patterns of the child. We can teach a three-year-old to read, but what

172

do the displacement of time demanded and the shift from the other experiences do to the long-term development of the child?

With the shift of emphasis moving more insistently towards the inclusion of more and more cognitive learning at increasingly earlier ages, there is a strong need to examine closely what the results of such an approach will be on human development. How valid is the claim that children of three and four can read and do arithmetic problems when the time and energy required for this to happen deprives those children of opportunities to dream, to experiment, to imagine, to create? What are the priorities regarding how children spend those precious minutes of early childhood, and who should determine them: parents? teachers? administrators? psychologists? And what is the goal of stressing cognitive learning at younger ages? If it is to produce people more able to function in a world filled with high technology and information, then another look needs to be taken. Fields such as engineering and medicine have recently conducted research which indicates that it is the well-rounded, more creative person who can withstand the high pressures that exist in the high tech society, and who can develop the strategies and solutions to meet the needs of that society. Students who have been narrowly prepared to enter a specialized field are, in fact, likely to be at a disadvantage when it comes to meeting the types of psychological and mental demands required in order to be successful over a period of time.

No one would claim that the arts are the final solution to the problems facing early childhood education. It cannot be denied, however, that there is a lack of balance existing in many educational programs used in preschools and elementary schools. The Smilansky researches, among others, provide evidence that when used as part of the core curriculum, the arts provide the important balance between the cognitive and the affective needs of young children. If they are to have the inner resources to make sense of the vast amount of knowledge that surrounds them, children must have time to experiment, to explore, to dream, to imagine: to simply "fool around" and delight in living. Children can be taught to read, but may have no interest in books, no understanding that entire worlds can exist in the pages once the meaning beyond the letters is understood and begins to touch the imagination and curiosity. To want to write, children must have an idea, a feeling, and the desire to share that idea or feeling through the medium of words. Unless they have meaningful experiences and personal thoughts to draw upon, children, when asked to write, can only respond with sparse, dull, uncaring compositions. The arts can help children break through the limited and rigid boundaries established when only one aspect of the human experience is known, that of the intellect which can accumulate facts and knowledge but cannot insist that they have meaning or importance. By engaging in the arts, children experience, interact, contemplate, integrate, discriminate, create — in other words, find ways to give meaning to those daily patterns of living which so easily can become monotonous and frustrating.

Arts education

> enriches the store of images that makes comprehension of concepts possible and comprehensive. This is the proper contribution of aesthetic education to language mastery, and if this is not basic to education, then it is difficult to imagine what would be. Aesthetic literacy is as basic as linguistic literacy.
> (Broudy, 1979)

Those schools which include the arts as an important part of their curriculum are places which, even on a casual visit, seem alive and humming with purposeful activity. Evidence of the richness of expression and communication is everywhere: hanging on walls, exhibited on shelves, and heard in the voices and seen on the faces of children and teachers. Words seem to achieve a deeper function, able to deliver messages which have multi-levels of meaning. Children seem to be treated as whole beings, with both intellectual and emotional needs and interests. Expressions of personal visions and of individual realities are encouraged. Because children become fully involved in the creative process required if those kinds of expressions are to be communicated through painting, sculpting, writing, singing, the integration between cognitive and affective learning is strengthened and increased. Ideas no longer need to exist in isolation and

174

have little personal meaning, but can be woven into the texture of each child's understanding.

How does clay fit into needs and interests of the child of the technological age? In this simple, pliable, ancient material can be found ways that the young child can begin the process of self-discovery and finding meaning in an often confusing world. Beyond the hardware and the software, the accumulation of facts and vast amounts of information, lies the sometimes forgotten but still important need to develop the senses. Recreating a three-dimensional world through a three-dimensional medium allows children to discover how they see, understand, and interpret the outward reality of life. At the same time, clay lends itself to the expression of those feelings and ideas which originate from the inward reality, from the imagination, that exists within each child. Thus, while exploring the outer realities, which are finite and often structured, the child can discover the inner world which has no limits, no boundaries. In learning to deal with both realities, the child begins to fulfill the potential of each human being to become fully-developed; caught not only in the grasp of measurable quantities and qualities, but those which give those quantities and qualities their purpose and meaning.

When used as a part of an integrated educational program, clay can contribute directly to the cognitive and affective learning of young children. This message, repeated and substantiated throughout this book, needs to reach the teachers, parents, and administrators who care about what happens to young children. Clay, as one medium with a proven and a significant contribution to make to the development of young children, should be included in the curriculum of every preschool and elementary school.

APPENDIX

Tests Developed by the Clay Project Staff

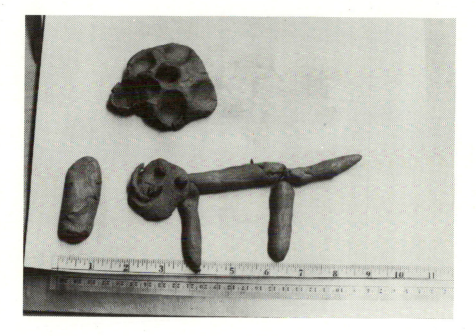

COGNITIVE CLAY SCALE

This scale is described
in Chapter Two; findings
are discussed in Chapter
Four.

EXPLANATION AND GUIDE FOR USING EVALUATION FORM, CLAY PROJECT: DOG

PROCESS EVALUATION:

This section should be scored by the person who is observing the child working in clay; it can be checked off as the child works or done immediately afterwards if the observer would prefer. This does not replace any descriptive notes that might need to be written as the child works.

+ The child did do the process described.
− The child did not do the process described.
0 Unobserved or unrecorded information.

CHILD'S FEELING ABOUT THE CLAY

1. Enjoyment: If the child seemed to enjoy his time with the clay the tester might indicate such things as verbal comments the child made about the clay in very positive ways; a description of the child's excitement about the clay and his enthusiasm about it, etc. Several positive aspects would result in a score of 7 or 6, then range downward to 2 or 1, which would indicate the child disliked the clay, said he didn't want to work with it, he sat there sullen or exceptionally shy and would not work.

2. Spontaneity: During the work process itself, if the child seemed to work with no difficulty, without asking for advice or help; seemed to know what he wanted to do and how he wanted to do it; did not seem to overplan his figure and stopped working when he felt he had what he wanted, this would indicate a high level of 7 or 6. On the other extreme, if the child constantly asked for help, seemed very unsure of himself, did not seem to know what he wanted to make or seemed very frustrated by the clay itself, then the score would be 1 or 2.

3. Satisfaction: If when the piece was finished the child clearly indicated by his expression or words to the tester that he really liked his pieces, that he was pleased with the results and thought he had done very well, then the score would be 7 or 6. If, how-

ever, the child seemed very disgusted with his results (even though he may have enjoyed the process of making the piece), then the score would be 1 or 2.

PRODUCT EVALUATION

Recognizability: This is to be scored on the basis of 10 photographs of children's clay dog. Each photograph is to be compared with the dog being evaluated. By comparing the child's work to one of the photographs, each of which is numbered according to the degree of recognizability, a close approximation of a comparable degree of recognizability can be assigned, and the chosen number should be circled on the form. Thus, if the child's work comes closest to resembling photograph number 6, then number 6 should be circled.

Number of Physical Details: If it can clearly be seen that one of the listed physical details is present in the child's dog, it should be checked off in the + column. If it is uncertain whether a detail is present, but the child has told the tester what the detail is and it is thus labeled so on the drawing form done by the tester, then that detail should be counted. If it is uncertain whether a detail is present and no labeling is present, or if the detail is not present, do not count that detail. The following details may need clarification:

1. *head:*   any clear indication of a head as separately handled from the body; that is, it should be clear that the child intended to make a head, not just another section of the body itself.

2. *body:*   any clear indication of a body as separately handled from the head; that is, it should be clear that the child intended to make a body, not just another section of the head.

181

3. *legs:*   any number of legs may be counted here as +; they need not come from the body to be counted.

4. *feet (paws):*   any clear indication the child tried to make feet, usually by adding or shaping clay at the ends of the legs, but can be counted as + if it is clear the child made feet but did not make legs.

5. *eyes:*   any suggestion of eyes, or one eye if head is sideways.

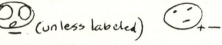

6. *mouth:*   any attempt to show a mouth.

7. *nose:*   any attempt to show a nose.

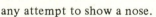

8. *neck:*   must be a clear departure from the head and body; does not need to be shaped.

9. *toes:*   any method of showing toes, no matter how many.

182

10. *toenails* (claws): any clear method of indicating toenails at the end of the feet or legs.

11. *ears:* any attempt to show ears; may be counted even if not on head if clearly meant to be ears.

12. *hair (fur):* any suggestion of hair or fur either on head, body, tail or legs using any methods.

13. *eyelashes:* any suggestion of eyelashes, but must be clearly indicated as separate from the eyes and along the top and/or bottom of the eyes, although not necessarily touching.

14. *pupil of eye:* any clear indication of the pupil or iris as distinct from the outline or shape of the eye. Should appear in both eyes if both are shown.

15. *shape of the eye:* if any attempt has been made either with the molding of the clay itself or drawing, to give the eye an oval shape rather than just a blob or circle.

16. *nostrils:* any indication the child tried to make nostrils; if no other nose suggestion is present, do not count unless it is obvious the child intended nostrils rather than some other physical or decorative detail.

17. *whiskers:* any attempt to show whiskers on the face of the dog; may also count + if the child made the little holes to indicate the placement of the whiskers around the face.

18. *shape of nose:* there are many possibilities here due to the wide variety in shapes of dogs' noses, but do not count + here unless it is very clear the child intended to give the nose some shape either by drawing on or shaping the clay.

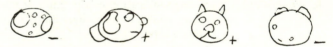

19. *shape of ears:* if the child tried to give the ears a definite shape rather than just making circles or blobs of clay on either side of the head.

20. *correct number of feet:* must show clearly four feet.

21. *correct number of legs:* must show clearly four legs.

22. *shape of body:* any clear indication the child tried to give the dog's body a shape rather than a circle or blob. Again, with the wide variety of dogs, many possibilities exist here.

23. *teeth:*   any clear indication the child tried to show teeth.

24. *shape of mouth:*   must clearly show the jaw line below and indicate in some way how the mouth is related to the nose.

25. *tongue:*   any clear indication the child tried to show a tongue.

26. *stomach:*   if the child clearly tried to indicate the stomach area as a well-defined detail, rather than having the same look at the top of the body as on the bottom in the 3-dimensional dog, for example, or by drawing on or shaping the clay in a 2-dimensional dog.

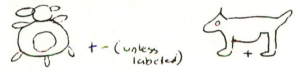

Number of Decorative Details: In any of the decorative details, if it is not clear if the detail is present and no label is present, do not count +. In order to count the collar, leash (chain), coat, bone, or buttons, they must be attached to the dog in some way: i.e., the collar around the dog's neck, the leash attached to the collar or even to the neck if no collar was attempted.

Correctly Placed Physical Details: For any of these, count + if the detail is clearly placed as described; count ± if the detail is nearly or closely placed as described; count − if the detail is not placed as described or is missing.

185

(if not labeled)

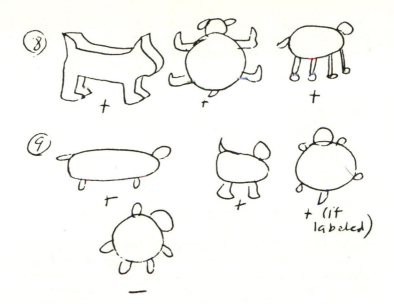

Proportions: In the dog, proportions vary to such an extent that it would be very difficult to state those which are correct in contrast to those which are not. Therefore, except for a few rather general proportions, this section will be limited in its application to the dog as interpreted by the very young child.

1. head to body: Score 4: Body is from 2 to 5 times larger than head.
   3: Body is slightly larger than head.
   2: Body and head are same size.
   1: Body is smaller than head.
   0: Not attempt or part missing.

2. eyes to head: Score 4: Eyes are 1/8 to 1/9 the size of the whole head.
   3: Eyes are larger then #4, but not more than 1/2 size of the whole head.
   2: Eyes are between 1/2 and 3/4 size of of whole head.
   1: Eyes are either 3/4 or up to size of whole head, or smaller than #4 in size (example would be two very tiny holes made with top of pencil or tool).
   0: Not attempted or part missing.

187

3D Concepts: In scoring 3D concepts, try to determine if the part named is clearly interpreted by the child in 3D manner: that is, the part is not flattened out in a cookie manner or simply outlined with strips of clay. Even if the figure is not standing, parts of that figure can be conceived by the child in 3D ways; for example, the head is often a round ball even if the rest of the figure is flattened out or outlined; in this case, the head would score +. If the head in this case were rounded but it is not completely clear if it was left round or somewhat flattened on the face and back of the head; or if there is any doubt as to whether it could be either 3D or 2D, score ±. If it is clear than the child did flatten out the clay or use clay to outline, then score 0.

TECHNIQUE EVALUATION

Textures: The child's use of textures involves any attempt made to show how a surface or materials might feel or look; it reveals the child's understanding that different types or kinds of materials are made of various kinds of substances each of which has its own characteristics. To show this, the higher level child may attempt to draw in the clay, press objects (stamp) the clay, add bits and pieces of clay or various combinations of these. In order to score accurately, it must be clear that the texturing attempts were deliberate, not accidental.

Score 2: This is the highest level, and if given for any detail listed would indicate that the child added bits or pieces of clay to the section mentioned and then used tool, objects, fingernails, etc., to show texture; or, if the clay figure of the dog has been pulled out of one lump of clay with no clay added, it would be clear that the clay was actually shaped or molded into the section to be scored *before* texturing was continued by the process described above.

Hair (fur): pieces or bits of clay are added to or pulled out of any parts of the dog and then drawn on or textured in some way to show hair pattern; or clay had clearly been pulled from the dog shape or molded from it in some way before texturing.

Collar: clay has been added to or pulled from the neck area of the dog, then given some clearly shown pattern or design to show what the collar might be made of.

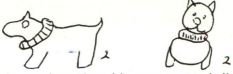

Leash (chain):   clay has been shaped in some way to indicate a leash; then the material of the leash or chain was indicated by use of a tool, fingernails, etc.

Coat: clay has been added to or pulled from (shaped) the dog to clearly show a coat (or sweater or jacket) on the dog; then some means of showing what that coat is made out of was attempted.

Score 1:

Hair: hair is drawn onto the surface of the dog without any additional clay being added or shaped; must clearly indicate a hair type pattern, not just random markings.

Collar: by means of a tool marking device, a collar has clearly been drawn into the clay, then given some type of texturing to show what the collar might be made of.

189

Leash (chain):   if no attempt was made to shape or mold the clay into the leash or chain but the chain was drawn into the clay surface (either directly on the side of the dog, for example, or into a flat piece of clay connected to the dog in some way) and then given some texturing.

Coat: by means of a tool or marking device, a coat has clearly been drawn into the clay, then given some type of texturing to show what materials the coat might be made of.

Score 0: No attempt made.

Connection of Parts: This section attempts to analyze what the child did with physical and decorative parts as far as methods used to include them in the figure. It is not expected that many preK and K children would score in the higher range of 4 through 7 until after intervention.

Score 0: Not attempted
Score 1: Not connected
      2: Just touching nearest part
      3: Overlapping connection; part is just laid at its end over the next part.
      4: Part smoothed onto figure; clay has been deliberately blended with the next part to create a continuous appearance in the dog.
      5: Was not connected because entire figure was shaped out of one piece of clay with the exception of the head, which was added.
      6: Was not connected because entire figure was shaped out of one piece of clay except for decorative details which were added.
      7: Was not connected because entire figure was shaped out of one piece.

190

Methods of Working with Entire Figure of Dog: In this section, checking off the characteristics of the three-dimensional aspects of the entire clay piece is all that is necessary. In number 8, Figure is almost standing, if the child resorted to any type of prop in order to get the dog to standup, or if he tried to get the figure of the dog to stand but couldn't and therefore made the dog sit up instead, score it here. However, if it is clear that the child intended from the first to have the dog sitting (back legs bent into correct position, front legs between back legs, for example), then score this as number 9, Figure is standing.

In number 7, Only part of the figure is standing, if the child tried to get the dog to stand but all the legs folded up or collapsed and the child let the dog's body and head remain upright but left the legs folded up or lying out flat around the body, then score it here. In a few cases, a child might deliberately plan to make a dog upright but in a lying down position, which also should be scored as 7, since this is a much easier way to make a 3D dog than either 8 or 9 would be.

In number 6, all parts of the figure are full (3D) but figure is lying down; the dog is made in a 2D manner, that is, flat on the working surface, but parts are all rounded even though they are seen only from the front; or if the child made the dog, tried to get it to stand, but could not so he laid it down on its side.

In number 5, figure has some full (3D) parts and some flat parts and is lying down; the dog is made in a 2D manner, that is, flat on the working surface, but one or more of the parts is rounded.

In number 4, all parts of the figure are flat and figure is lying down; the same position as in number 6 is true except all parts are made in a 2D manner.

In number 3, figure is outlined with clay but head is full (3D); coils of clay or small pieces of clay are used to show just the outline of the figure (including both physical and decorative parts quite often), but the head is done in a rounded (3D) manner.

In number 2, entire figure is outlined with clay, the same description as in number 3 is true, except even the head is outlined.

In number 1, the child did not try to make a dog.

PROCESS EVALUATION: CHILD'S METHODS OF WORKING WITH CLAY

In this section, a score of + would indicate that the child did do the process described; − would indicate he did not; 0 would indicate that no description of this was available.

CHILD'S FEELINGS ABOUT THE CLAY

1. Enjoyment: If the child seemed to enjoy his time with the clay the tester might indicate such things as verbal comments the child made about the clay in very positive ways; a description of the child's excitement about the clay and his enthusiasm about it, etc. Several positive aspects would result in a score of 7 or 6, then range downward to 2 or 1, which would indicate the child disliked the clay, said he didn't want to work with it, he sat there sullen or exceptionally shy and would not work.

2. Spontaneity: During the work process itself, if the child seemed to work with no difficulty, without asking for advice or help; seemed to know what he wanted to do and how he wanted to do it; did not seem to overplan his figure and stopped working when he felt he had what he wanted, this would indicate a high level of 7 or 6. On the other extreme, if the child constantly asked for help, seemed very unsure of himself, did not seem to know what he wanted to make or seemed very frustrated by the clay itself, then the score would be 1 or 2.

3. Satisfaction: If when the piece was finished the child clearly indicated by his expression or words to the tester that he really liked his piece, that he was pleased with the results and thought he had done very well, then the score would be 7 or 6. If, however, the child seemed very disgusted with his results (even though he may have enjoyed the process of making the piece), then the score would be 1 or 2.

192

PRODUCT EVALUATION

Recognizability: This is to be scored on the basis of 10 photographs of children's clay figures. Each photograph is to be compared with the figure being evaluated. By comparing the child's work to one of the photographs, each of which is numbered according to the degree of recognizability, a close approximation of a comparable degree of recognizability can be assigned, and the chosen number should be circled on the form. Thus, if the child's work comes closest to resembling photograph number 6, then number 6 should be circled.

Number of Physical Details: If it can clearly be seen that one of the listed physical details is present in the child's figure, it should be checked off in the + column. If it is uncertain whether a detail is present, but the child has told the tester what the detail is and it is thus labeled so on the drawing form done by the tester, then that detail should be counted. If it is uncertain whether a detail is present and no labeling is present, or if the detail is not present, do not count that detail. The following details may need clarification:

5. *eyes:*   any suggestion of eyes, or one eye if head is sideways.

3. and 4. *legs and arms:* if only one leg or one arm is present, cross off the *s* on the form and still score +.

8. *neck:*   any clear indication of the neck as distinct from the head and body.

9. *hands:*   must be clearly represented, apart from arm and fingers. Clay should be a little thicker between the arm and fingers to represent the palm or back of hand, and should appear on both hands if both are shown.

10. *feet:*   any means of showing feet, either from a front view or side.

11. *fingers:*   any obvious method of making fingers no matter how many.

12. *toes:*   any method of showing toes, no matter how many.

13. *knees:*   if not labeled, it should be obvious that child made circles of clay in the middle part of each leg, or drew with tool to indicate knee part.

14. *hips:*   If not labeled, it should be obvious that child made circles of clay on either side of lower part of body, or on back if figure is 3D.

15. *ears:*   any clear indications of ears on either side of head or one ear if head is sideways.

16. *hair:*   any method of showing hair, including pieces of clay on top of head, coils of clay draped around head, or drawing or texturing hair on top and or sides of head. If it is clear child intended to have the head bald (either by tester's label or just a little hair is shown around each ear) score +.

17. *beard:* any method of showing hair around chin and mouth area; using pieces or coils of clay or texture or drawing. If it looks like whiskers or unshaven lower face, score +.

18. *eyebrows:* any method of showing eyebrows, but must be obviously separate from the eyes and over the top of both eyes if shown.

19. *eyelashes:* any methods of showing eyelashes, but must be obviously separate from the eyes and along the top and or bottom of the eyes, although not necessarily touching.

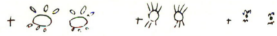

20. *pupil of eye:* any clear indication of the pupil or iris as distinct from the outline or shape of the eye. Should appear in both eyes if both are shown.

21. *shape of eye:* if any attempt has been made by child either with the molding of the clay itself or drawing, to give the eye an oval shape rather than just a blob or circle.

22. *nostrils:* any indication the child tried to make nostrils either at the bottom of a drawn (outlined) nose or shaped nose; count only if there are 2 shown unless side view.

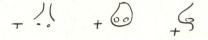

23. *shape of nose:* if the nose is shown wider at the bottom and either by use of drawing on the clay or shaping the clay the nose is shown as starting just above or at the level of the eyes and either curving or sloping down to the base or tip.

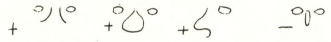

24. *lips:* any method of showing the mouth has lips, either by coils or drawing on the clay; must show two, both top and bottom lip.

25. *chin:* should be clear child meant to show chin either by the way he shaped the clay or else by drawing on the clay.

26. *shape of ears:* if the child tried to show the shape of the ear rather than just a blob, circle or drawn circle, or hole in clay.

28. *shape of hands:* if the hands have been shaped as in 9, but the opposition of the thumb from the fingers is clearly shown.

29. *shoulders:*   any clear indication that the child formed shoulders at the top of the body; just rounded corners do not count if the body still has the appearance of a circle or oval. The width of the top of the body should be wider than the lower part, with the joining of the arms as part of the width,

30. *shape of feet:*   if attempts have been made to show the feet with heel and with length greater than its height.

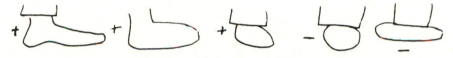

31. *shape of body:*   any clear indication the child tried to show a waist by indenting the clay, tapering the body from more width at top to narrowness near center area. In female figure indications of breast area being wider would count.

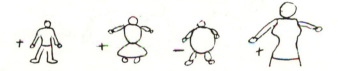

32. *style of hair:*   any attempt by the child to actually give the hair shape by use of side burns, bangs, piled up curls with hair also indicated by ears in some way, or by clearly indicating the hair is parted, combed or brushed by either lines drawn in the clay or by added or pieces of clay which are small enough to show the style being worked out or else they have been textured in some way to show hair lines.

Number of Decorative Details: In any of the decorative details, if it is not clear if the detail is present and no label is available, do not count +. In 26. and 27., the purse and umbrella must be held by the figure in some way to count.

Correctly placed Physical Details: For any of these, count + if the detail is clearly placed as described; count ± if the detail is nearly or closely placed as described; count − if the detail is not placed as described. In number 4, for example, the arms cannot be counted as joined correctly if they came out from the middle of the body or if the body and arms have been carved out of one piece with the arms the same thickness as the body. If the child has not indicated shoulders, then it must be clear the arms are joined at the top of either side of the body, not at the neck or head, and only number 3 would be scored +, not number 4.

198

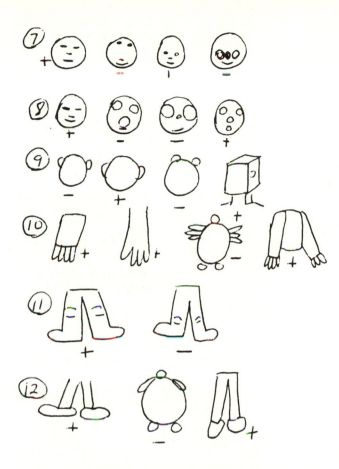

Proportions: Proportions are not always easy to determine, but for the very
young child not many have as yet been recognized so scoring in
this section may seem to be very low. In the scoring, the ideal
proportions of 5 will be achieved by few if any children, and
even 4 would have few checks in most cases; 3 indicates what
could be considered average in the concept of proportion for this
age group in most cases.

1. head to body: *Score 5.* Body is 3 to 4 times larger than head.
                          4. Body is 2 to 3 times larger than head.
                          3. Body is slightly larger than head.
                          2. Body is same size as head.

199

1. Body is smaller than head.

0. Not attempted or part missing.

2. legs to body: Score   *5.* Legs are slightly longer than body.

4. Legs are same length as body.

3. Legs are about half the size of the body.

2. Legs are less than 1/2 the size of the body.

1. Legs are less than 1/4 size of the body.

0. Not attempted or part missing.

3. arms to body: Score *5.* Arms are length of figure from top of body to just above the knees.

4. Arms are same length as body.

3. Arms are about half the size of the body.

2. Arms are less than 1/2 the size of the body.

1. Arms are less than 1/4 the size of the body.

0. Not attempted or part missing.

4. eyes to head: Score *5.* Eyes are 1/8 to 1/9 the size of the whole head.

4. Eyes are between 1/4 and 1/8 of the whole head.

3. Eyes are between 1/2 and 1/4 of the whole head.

2. Eyes are between 3/4 and 1/2 of the whole head.

1. Eyes are either 3/4 or larger than head or smaller than 1/9, as in score of 5.

0. Not attempted or part missing.

5. nose to head: Score *5.* Nose is about 1/5 the size of the whole head.

4. Nose is about 1/4 the size of the whole head.

3. Nose is about 1/3 the size of the whole head.

2. Nose is about 1/2 the size of the whole head.

200

1. Nose is over 1/2 the size of the whole head or smaller than 1/5 as in score of 5.

6. mouth to head:

Score 5. Mouth scores same as eyes to head, see #4.

7. hand to arm: Score 5. Hand is 1/3 the size of the arm.
4. Hand is 1/4 the size of the arm.
3. Hand is 1/2 the size of the arm.
2. Hand is 3/4 the size of the arm.
1. Hand is the same size as arm or larger.
0. Not attempted or part missing.

8. fingers to hand: 5. Fingers the same length as hand.
4. Fingers 3/4 the size of the hand.
3. Fingers slightly larger than hand.
2. Fingers 1/2 the size of the hand.
1. Fingers smaller than 1/2 or much larger than hand.
0. Not attempted or part missing.

9. foot to leg: Score 5. Foot is 1/3 the size of the leg.
4. Foot is 1/4 the size of the leg.
3. Foot is 1/2 the size of the leg.
2. Foot is almost as large as leg.
1. Foot is same size as leg or larger.
0. Not attempted or part missing.

10. ears to head: Score the same as hand to arm, #7.

11. neck to head: Score the same as hand to arm, #7.

12. toes to feet: Score 5. Toes are between 1/4 and 1/3 the size of the feet.
4. Toes are between 1/2 and 1/4 the size of the feet.
3. Toes are between 1/8 and 1/4 the size of the feet.
2. Toes are almost the same size as feet.
1. Toes are larger than the foot or smaller than 1/8 of the foot.
0. Not attempted or part missing.

3D Concepts: In scoring 3D concepts, try to determine if the part named is clearly interpreted by the child in a 3D manner; that is, the part is not flattened out in a cookie manner or simply outlined with strips of clay. Even if the figure is not standing, parts of the figure can be conceived by the child in 3D ways; for example, the head is often a round ball even if the rest of the figure is flattened out and outlined; in this case, the head would score +. If the head in this case were rounded but it is not completely clear if it was left round or somewhat flattened on the face and back of the head, or if there is any doubt as to whether it could be either 3D or 2D, score ±. If it is clear that the child did flatten our the clay or use clay to outline, then score −.

TECHNIQUE EVALUATION:

Textures: The child's use of textures involves any attempt made to show how a surface or material might feel or look; it reveals the child's understanding that different types or kinds of materials are made of various kinds of substances each of which has its own characteristics. To show this, the higher level child may attempt to draw in the clay, press objects (stamp) the clay, add bits and pieces of clay or various combinations of these. In order to score accurately, it must be clear that the texturing attempts were deliberate, not accidental.

Score 2: This is the highest level, and with each area (hair, eyebrows, etc.), would indicate that the child added bits or pieces of clay to the section and then used tool, objects, fingernails, etc., to show texture; or, if the clay figure has been pulled out of one lump of clay with no clay added, it should be clear that the clay was actually shaped or molded into the section to be scored *before* texturing was continued by the process described above. Examples in each section of a score of 2 would be:

1. *Hair:*   Pieces or bits of clay are added to or pulled out of the head and then drawn on or textured in some way to show curls, braids, parts, combing lines, afro, etc.

OUT LINE   TYPE

202

2. *Eyebrows:*   Same techniques used to show hair to indicate eyebrows above each eye; typical example would be use of a narrow coil which is added above each eye and then textured to show hair lines.

3. *Skirt or bottom of dress:* Clay is added or shaped to show folds and then texture is used to indicate the type of material or designs which are part of the material itself.

4. *Belt:*   Clay clearly has been shaped or added around the waist area to resemble a type of belt and then some method of showing what the belt is made of or designs on the belt have been indicated; the buckle should be present or some method of fastening the belt.

5. *Hat:*   Any clear attempt to show a hat sitting on top of the head or being held in the person's hand, plus attempts to show what the hat is made out of and/or what some of the parts of the hat are made of such as texture of the hatband, the feathers, flowers, etc.

203

6. *Pants:*   Any attempt to show clearly what the pants are made out of and should indicate the clay has been shaped or added to indicate the material of the pants, then textured.

7. *Jacket:*   Same as 6.

8. *Top of dress or blouse:* Same as 6; should include some neckline, either a collar or edge around the neck clearly shown; if sleeveless, edges should look finished.

9. *Beard:*   Same as 1.

10. *Shirt:*   Same as 8.

11. *Vest:*   Should be obviously separately textured from the shirt or blouse beneath and may show some method of fastening and have labels or a finished looking edge; textures could be all over type patterns or lines of any deliberate nature.

Score 1: On this level, the child does show texture, but he does so by drawing the textures on the surface of the clay with no attempt to build up the shape first; also, the textures are usually less detailed and sophisticated.

1. *Hair:*   Hair is drawn onto the surface of the head; must be clearly a deliberate attempt to show the texture of the hair by indicating combing line, curls, bangs, etc.

2. *Eyebrows:*   Must be indicated by more than a single line drawn above each eye to count as texture; must clearly indicate above each eye wavy, curly or straight lines in each eyebrow.

3. *Skirt or bottom of dress:* Lines of some kind are clearly indicated to show folds in the materials or else designs and/or kind of material are clearly indicated; just showing one large flower in the center of the skirt area would not count; an all-over pattern or design would count.

4. *Belt:*   Clear indications of a belt drawn around the waist area with some method used to show materials in the belt or designs on the belt; buckle or some method of fastening should be present.

5. *Hat:*   May be drawn on the surface of the head itself but should have obvious sections of a hat such as hatband, flowers, feathers, etc.

6. *Pants:*   Any attempt clearly made to show by drawing or stamping clay that the pants have a type of material or design (all-over kind), but done directly on the leg itself with no attempt to show shape of the pants first.

7. *Jacket:*   Same as 6.

8. *Top of dress or blouse:* Same as 6; drawn right on top of body with no attempt to show a shape first; should include some neckline, either a collar or edge drawn around the neck; if sleeveless, edges should look finished.

9. *Beard:*   Same as 1.

10. *Shirt:*   Same as 8.

11. *Vest:*   Should be obviously drawn on the body separately from the blouse or shirt underneath and show some method of fastening, with either lapels or a finished looking neck edge; textures could be all over type patterns or lines of a deliberate nature.

Score 0:   No attempt made.

206

Connection of Parts: This section attempts to analyze what the child did with physical and decorative parts as far as methods used to include them in the figure. It is not expected that many preK and K children would score in the higher range of 4 through 7 until after intervention.

Score
1: Not connected
2: Just touching
3: Overlapping connections; part is just laid at the end over the next.
4: Part smoothed onto figure; clay has been deliberately blended to create a continuous appearance in the clay figure.
5: Was not connected because entire figure was shaped out of one piece with the exception of the head.
6: Was not connected because entire figure was shaped out of one piece except for decorative details.
7: Was not connected because entire figure was shaped out of one piece.

Methods of Working with Entire Figure: In this section, simply checking off the characteristics of the three-dimensional aspects of the entire clay piece is all that is necessary. In number 8, "Figure is almost standing", if the child resorted to any type of prop to get the figure to stand or if he had to make the figure sit because he couldn't get it to stand this would be checked here. However, if the child deliberately intended to make his figure in a position other than standing and the figure is completely shown in a full, 3D manner, it should be counted in number 9, with the exception of lying down figures, scored in 6. In number 7, if the child managed to prop or angle the figure so that it is upright from the waist up or the knees up and it is not sitting (see number 8), it is counted here. Outlining with the clay might involve using coils of clay to simply show the outline of the figure, or small pieces of clay might be used to make a sort of narrow wall effect to do the same thing.

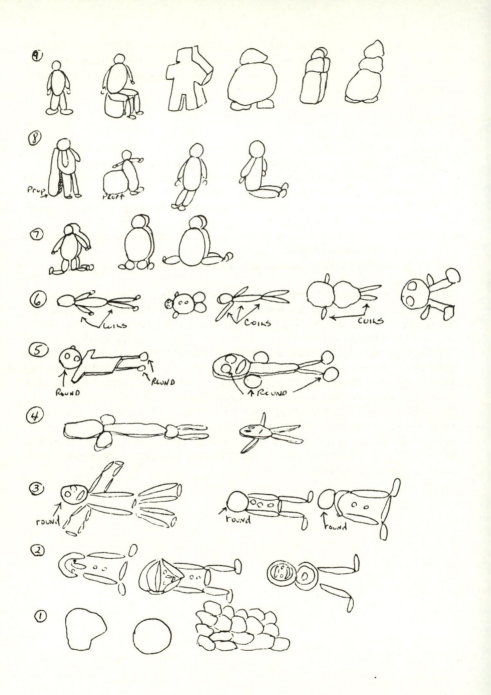

(Please circle correct information in all
sections of this form requiring selection
of one answer from several possibilities.)

PRE-INTERVENTION   POST-INTERVENTION

FREE   PERSON   DOG

CLAY

Name of Child _____

Computer Number _____

Sex: M___ F___

Ethnic Group: 1 2 3 4 5

School _____
              Number (   )

School Cluster Number _____

Teacher _____
              Number (   )

Evaluator _____
              Number (   )

Intervention Group:
     1. Control   4. Discussion
     2. Enrichment A
     3. Enrichment B   5. Technique

Date of Test _____
           Yr.   Mo.   Da.

Date of Birth _____
           Yr.   Mo.   Da.

Age: Years_____   Months _____

Total Months_____

Grade: Pre-Kindergarten   Kindergarten

Time: Begin _____   End _____ = TOTAL _____

PART I

PROCESS EVALUATION: CHILD'S METHODS OF WORKING WITH CLAY

A. In this section, a sequential record of the process used by the child as he engages with
the clay is to be written by the evaluator. (Include any interactions with testor).

    1.

    2.

    3.

    4.

5.

6.

7.

8.

9.

10.

11.

12.

B (1) Verbal Activities of the Child: Please check appropriate boxes.

R = Related to clay.
NR = Not related to clay

	+		O
	R	NR	
4. Talked almost the entire time while working with clay without the evaluator talking to him.			
3. Talked a lot on his own while working with clay but worked quietly part of the time.			
2. Talked only when spoken to by evaluator and very little on his own while working with clay.			
1. Did not talk at all even when evaluator asked questions (child might have used body movements such as shaking head instead of words.)			
B (2) Talked or sang to the clay while working.			

C. Please check appropriate box that most closely fits the child's method of working with the clay.

WHOLE/WHOLE:

	+	O
1 Left clay as lump; did not form into any shape.		
2 Left clay as lump; named it.		
3 Left clay as lump but pounded into shape and named it.		
4 Left clay as lump but pounded into shape and did not name it.		

PARTS/WHOLE:

5 Pulled or pinched off pieces from lump of clay and connected them together as he worked.		
6 Pulled or pinched off pieces from lump of clay, left all or most parts separate until end, then connected them together.		
7 Cut off pieces (using clay tools), then connected them back together.		

WHOLE/PARTS:

8 (Left clay as lump and put part(s)(poked or punched or drew) on lump.		
9 Pulled or pinched all parts out from whole (did not separate parts from initial lump).		
10 Pulled or pinched parts out as in (9) except for one or two additional separate parts added.		
11 Carved with tools from one piece of clay (did not separate parts from initial piece).		

PARTS/PARTS:

12 Pulled off pieces, rounded or shaped these, but never connected them.		
13 Pulled off pieces, no rounding or shaping, no connecting.		
14 Cut off pieces with clay tool but never connected them.		

D. Methods of Connecting Parts: Please check appropriate box(es) that describe most connections of parts. (Check more than one if equally used.)

1 Did not make parts or he drew, punched, or poked parts.	
2 Not connected to each other.	
3 Just touching each other.	
4 Combination of just touching and overlapping each other.	
5 Overlapping each other; parts are laid at the ends over or under other parts.	
6 Parts are connected together by some kind of pinching.	
7 Parts are smoothed together; clay has been deliberately blended to create a continuous appearance in the clay figure or shape.	

E. Process Patterns: Circle a pattern if it seems to apply to this child's way of working
with clay in this particular task.

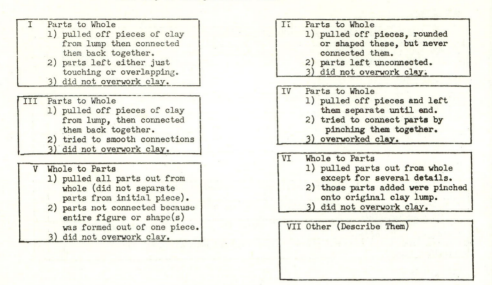

I   Parts to Whole
1) pulled off pieces of clay
from lump then connected
them back together.
2) parts left either just
touching or overlapping.
3) did not overwork clay.

II   Parts to Whole
1) pulled off pieces, rounded
or shaped these, but never
connected them.
2) parts left unconnected.
3) did not overwork clay.

III   Parts to Whole
1) pulled off pieces of clay
from lump, then connected
them back together.
2) tried to smooth connections
3) did not overwork clay.

IV   Parts to Whole
1) pulled off pieces and left
them separate until end.
2) tried to connect parts by
pinching them together.
3) overworked clay.

V   Whole to Parts
1) pulled all parts out from
whole (did not separate
parts from initial piece).
2) parts not connected because
entire figure or shape(s)
was formed out of one piece.
3) did not overwork clay.

VI   Whole to Parts
1) pulled parts out from whole
except for several details.
2) those parts added were pinched
onto original clay lump.
3) did not overwork clay.

VII Other (Describe Them)

F. Child's Feelings About The Clay: Check number for each item which best suits child's
feelings about clay. Do not score until child is finished
with clay because child's feelings may change during process.

	High	7	6	5	4	3	2	1	Low
1. Enjoyment: Child seemed to enjoy working with clay during process; he was confident, relaxed, able to concentrate, involved with the act of creating.									
2. Spontaneity: Child worked easily and with confidence during process; child did not appear to be trying to please the adult or simply fulfill an assignment; he became involved in the process of clay to the extent that he was able to let his own feelings and ideas evolve in a free and open manner.									
3. Satisfaction: Child seemed to be satisfied with his piece at conclusion of process; he expressed his satisfaction by his verbal or facial expressions.									

PRODUCT EVALUATION

A. Recognizability:

Compare this product with the drawings in the recognizability scale. Decide
which of the ten categories most nearly resembles the product; circle number.

Low   1   2   3   4   5   6   7   8   9   10   High

B. Physical Details:

After child finishes his product, look at it and attempt to identify as many
details as possible; give these a plus. If some details are not clear enough
for you to identify, ask the child what the detail is by pointing to it and
asking, "What is this?" In the appropriate box next to the detail that you
asked the child about, indicate that you did ask him the question, and score the
detail a plus if he identified it; a 0 if he did not, or if he says the detail is
nothing. Don't ask the child to describe or tell you about his product in a
general way.

	tester asked child	+	0		tester asked child	+	0
1. head/body comb.				31. hands			
2. head				32. fingers			
3. body				33. elbows			
4. eyes				34. shape of eye			
5. mouth				35. shape of nose			
6. lips				36. shape of ears			
7. nose				37. shape of hands (paws)			
8. chin				38. shape of body			
9. ears				39. shape of feet			
10. hair				40. shape of mouth			
11. neck				41. style of hair			
12. eyebrows				42. correct number of fingers			
13. eyelashes				43. correct number of legs			
14. eyelids				44. correct number of feet			
15. pupil of eye				45. mustache or whiskers			
16. nostrils				46. beard			
17. teeth				47. penis (child's word sub.)			
18. tongue				48. tail			
19. shoulders				49.			
20. stomach				50.			
21. waist				51.			
22. hips				52.			
23. legs				53.			
24. feet				54.			
25. ankles				55.			
26. toes				56.			
27. toenails				57.			
28. knees				58.			
29. arms				59			
30. wrist				60.			

TOTAL _____

(DOG)

C. Number of Decorative Details (See instructions for physical details).

	asked	+	0			asked	+	0
1. collar					9.			
2. leash					10.			
3. chain					11.			
4. bone (attached)					12.			
5. toy (attached)					13.			
6.					14.			
7.					15.			
8.					16.			

TOTAL _____

D. Number of Background Details (See instructions for physical details).

	asked	+	0			asked	+	0
1. dog house					9.			
2. bone					10.			
3. bowl or dish					11.			
4. fence					12.			
5. bed					13.			
6. blanket					14.			
7. rug					15.			
8. toy					16.			

TOTAL _____

Total of number of physical details _____
Total of number of decorative details _____
Total of number of background details _____

TOTAL _____

E. Correctly Placed Physical Details: Please mark each of the following according to your judgment: + (plus) means the detail is placed correctly; 0 (zero) means the detail is not placed correctly or is missing.

	+	0
1. head on top front end of body		
2. head on top of neck		
3. eyes placed on head		
4. nose between eyes and mouth		
5. mouth below nose		
6. ears on sides or top of head		
7. legs joined to body beneath or at lower sides		
8. feet or paws at ends of legs		
9. toes or claws at ends of feet.		
10. tail at back of body		

TOTAL _____

(DOG)

F. Proportions:

Before filling out the boxes below, indicate on a scale of 1-10 how in your judgment this child understood proportions of a dog, or how well he was able to relate the various parts of a dog as regards size to each other.

Low   1   2   3   4   5   6   7   8   9   10   High

Check the number in each section which corresponds _most_ with the product being evaluated.

Body to head

4. Body is larger than head.	
3. Body and head are the same size.	
2. Body is smaller than head.	
1. Not attempted or part missing.	

Eye(s) to head

4. Eye(s) 1/4 size of head or smaller.	
3. Eye(s) between 1/4 and 1/2 size of head.	
2. Eye(s) 1/2 size of head or larger.	
1. Not attempted or part missing.	

TOTAL _____

G. Whole Figure or Shape:

Check the description which best describes the product being evaluated.

7. Figure of shape is upright (vertical) unsupported by props, etc.	
6. Figure or shape is upright (vertical) but has some support.	
5. Part of figure or shape is upright (vertical) and part is lying down (horizontal).	
4. Figure or shape is lying down (horizontal).	
3. Clay is upright (vertical) but was not organized into a figure or shape.	
2. Clay is lying down (horizontal) but was not organized into a figure or shape.	
1. Child would not work with clay.	

TOTAL _____

H. Three Dimensional Details:

Check the details listed as to whether or not each is by itself three dimensional (3D), in other words existing in space from all angles, not flattened on the back in a cookie like fashion, drawn with a tool, punched into the clay, etc. If figure or shape is horizontal, be sure that the head, body, legs and arms were left rounded all around the part, not just on the top.

		+	0			+	0
1. head/body comb.				25. toes			
2. head				26. toenails			
3. body				27. knees			
4. eyes				28. arms			
5. mouth				30. wrist			
6. lips				31. hands			
7. nose				32. fingers			
8. chin				33. elbows			
9. ears				34. mustache or whiskers			
10. hair				35. beard			
11. neck				36. penis(child's word sub.)			
12. eyebrows				37. tail			
13. eyelashes				38.			
14. eyelids				39.			
15. pupil of eye				40.			
16. teeth				41.			
17. tongue				42.			
18. shoulders				43.			
19. stomach				44.			
20. waist				45.			
21. hips				46.			
22. legs				47.			
23. feet				48.			
24. ankles							

Total Number of 3D Details _____

Total Correctly Placed Physical Details _____
Total Score Proportions _____
Total Score Whole Figure or Shape _____
Total Number of 3D Details _____

TOTAL _____

I. Size of Figure or Shape:
   (G. In Free)

Height of figure or total organized product as measured from top (including hat, hair, etc.) to bottom; or height of highest completed part if parts were never assembled or organized. (If child used working surface for part of product, measure from bottom of lowest part of clay to highest, as shown:)

Height _____

Width of figure or total organized product as measured at widest point; or width of the same part used to determine height. (If child used working surface for part of product, measure from clay used farthest on either side as shown:)

Width _____

(Multiply Height x Width) =   Square _____

PART III

TECHNIQUE EVALUATION

A. Overall Technique Evaluation:

After reading through the process used by the child and looking at the product, if any, of the child (either the product itself if available or the photograph and/or drawing of the product), try to form a judgment of how well you think the child understood and controlled the medium of clay. In other words, did the child seem to realize clay has its own unique characteristics and that by utilizing these, expression through the clay medium is possible? The less well the child did in this area the lower his number score; the better he did the higher his number score. Please circle the number you believe comes the closest.

Low   1   2   3   4   5   6   7   8   9   10   High

B. Textures:

The child's use of textures involves any attempt made to show how a surface or material might feel or look. Textures can be made with drawings in the clay, pressing objects into the clay (stamping), adding bits and pieces of clay, etc. In order to score accurately, it must be clear that the texturing attempts were deliberate, not accidental. In scoring, check those items listed that did have texture, and add any additional items. If you know how the child textured the item, indicate by checking the appropriate box or write in how it was done if necessary.

	+	0	fingernail	tool	stamp	other (describe)
1. hair						
2. eyebrows						
3. mustache or whiskers						
4. beard						
5. jacket						
6. coat						
7. hat						
8. dress						
9. skirt						
10. shirt or blouse						
11. shoes						
12. socks						
13. belt						
14. necktie						
15. collar						
16.						
17.						
18.						
19.						
20.						

Total Number of Textures_____

C. Use of Clay Tools:

Please check this section only if the child did use clay tools in making his clay product.

	YES	NO
1. DID the child use a tool at the beginning to cut the clay?		
2. DID the child use a tool during the process of making the figure?		
3. IF YES for #2, was the tool used for texturing the clay?		
4. IF YES for #2, was the tool used for connecting or smoothing parts together?		
5. DID the child use more than one type of clay tool?		
6. DID the child try to substitute clay tools for parts of the figure itself?		

SCULPTURAL CLAY SCALE

This scale is described in Chapter Two; findings are discussed in Chapter Four.

A SCALE FOR THE ANALYSIS OF YOUNG CHILDREN'S CLAY SCULPTURE

DIRECTIONS FOR SCORING

In the application of the scale to individual clay pieces, scoring is done for each subtest using the following scale:

Low   1   2   3   4   5   6   7   High

If scores have been kept for previous products, it is possible to compare these with scores being made on current works. If change *between* products is to be examined, a slightly different scale can be applied for each subtest:

−3   A striking loss has occurred between the previous and present product in the area being analyzed.

−2   A significant loss has occurred between the previous and present product in the area being analyzed.

−1   A slight loss has occurred between the previous and present product in the area being analyzed.

0   No change has occurred between the previous and present product in the area being analyzed.

1   A slight gain has occurred between the previous and present product in the area being analyzed.

2   A significant gain has occurred between the previous and present product in the area being analyzed.

3   A striking gain has occurred between the previous and present product in the area being analyzed.

Since both the scoring used to evaluate change and the individual scoring of products use a scale with a seven point spread, it is possible to use one scoring as a check against the other. For example, if a child has made Product A, then several weeks later Product B is compared to A, two individual scores can be given for each product plus a change score when the two products are compared with each other. By subtracting the score of Product B from A, a similar score to that found in the change score should be gotten. Therefore, if a child received a score of 4 for Product A and a score of 6 for Product B, the difference is a gain of 2 points, or +2. If the change score for the two products compared was also a +2, it could be a further support for the validity of the analysis.

It is important to remember that the highest rating possible be given to the clay product, but that the clay piece should not be rated higher than it deserves for reasons which have nothing to do with the actual product. Examples of such reasons might be: "Well, I just like it!" "He really tried hard on this piece." "She has had such a hard day today, I'll give her a break." While all of these may be legitimate reasons for sympathy, they are not justification for sculptural scores. If the Sculptural Scale is to be correctly used it will be directed only towards the product, not the child. Thus the child will not be labeled or categorized. The purpose of the Scale is to give the teacher insight into how a child or group of children interact with the medium of clay, and the analyzation of the product is the means to that end. In this way a teacher may become aware of how children can be helped as they move from one level to the next.

In the scoring levels described for each of the Sculptural Scale subtests deliberate overlapping has been built in; in this way it is hoped that greater amounts of differentiation can occur. The general explanation for each criteria can therefore be arranged broadly into seven levels, but within each level can exist characteristics which can combine together in a variety of ways. Some of these combinations will tend to support higher or lower scoring within a level. Experience with the application of the Scale will clarify the range of scoring possibilities.

EXPLANATION OF TERMS

OVERALL

Before analyzing the clay piece by applying the five subtests that follow, look at the work in its totality and attempt to arrive at an overall evaluation, a first impression, which will indicate your opinion or judgment of that clay piece as a sculptural object.

Low   1   2   3   4   5   6   7   High

SURFACE TREATMENT

In analyzing the product for this aspect, it is important to distinguish between what the child seemed to do deliberately and what may have happened accidentally. Although the accidental treatment may in fact add to the overall appearance of the piece, it should not score as high as treatment which has been thought through and skillfully handled. In clay work of young children in the beginning stages of clay work few children go beyond the accidental texturing or occasional marking of the surface.

Score

7
6
Product was deliberately smoothed or given a rough or bumpy texture; clay was given a decorative or design pattern. The treatment complements and is integrated with the concept being presented so that the final result is one of variety and interest without distracting from the total piece.

6
5
Product was deliberately smoothed or given a rough or bumpy texture; *or* clay was given a decorative or design pattern. In either case the treatment seems to complement the concept being presented. However, the variety and interest which the treatment provides does distract somewhat from the final result.

4
Product is treated as above except that little integration with the the subject matter is seen; or the treatment is not enough to indicate it actually does complement the concept being presented.

3
2
Product has a rough or bumpy and/or smoothed surface but in a haphazard, accidental appearing manner. The final effect may help improve the final result even though it was not planned to do so.

1
Product shows no sign it has been treated in any way on the surface; it seems to be in its natural state with no surface interest at all.

SCULPTURAL SPACE

In analyzing the product for this aspect, it is important to look for evidence that the child understood the possibilities of extending the clay in more than one direction. Even in a basically horizontal piece, there should be some evidence of the concept requiring such a limitation rather than the child being unaware of other possibilities. The same thing would be true of a basically vertical object. In addition to the horizontal and vertical possibilities, does the child seem to be able to deal with or utilize the positive and negative potentials of the clay? For example, does he see the clay as only a solid, or does he attempt to open up sections?

222

Score

7 Product has both horizontal and vertical interest; it has been devel-
6 oped to about the fullest extent within the limits of the concept
being presented. In addition, there is some attempt to utilize positive and negative space. The use of space is integrated with the subject or idea; the sense of space supports the final object completely.

6 Product has both horizontal and vertical interest; some use of pos-
5 itive and negative space may or may not be present. In whatever
spacial treatment is used, the sense of space supports the final object but not to the fullest extent.

4 Product has either primarily vertical or horizontal interest, neither of which seems to completely assist in the development and presentation of the final idea or concept.

3 Product shows little understanding of how space can be utilized;
2 basically it is a flat presentation with little integration between
subject or concept and the sense of space.

1 Product shows no understanding of how space can be utilized; basically it is a flat presentation which seems to be in an unfinished or disjointed condition.

UNITY OF CONCEPTS

In analyzing the product for this aspect, it is important to concentrate on the manner in which the concepts or ideas are arranged or organized as they are made evident through the medium of clay. It is possible to go from an extreme of too much information (many details, a great many parts) which is poorly organized to the opposite extreme of too little information (details and parts are so few that the concept or idea has no support).

Score

7 Product shows strong evidence of organizational ability: parts seem
6 integrated into the concept or idea being presented. The total im-
pression of the piece is one of wholeness, although any number of parts and details could be present. Enough information is provided through the presentation to convey clearly the concept or idea.

6 Product shows some evidence of organizational ability; parts are
5 somewhat integrated into the concept or idea being presented. The
total impression ot the piece is not quite one of wholeness; either not quite enough information or a little too much is given through the clay medium.

Product shows little evidence of organizational ability; parts are not
4 well integrated into the concept or idea being presented. The total
impression of the piece is not quite one of wholeness; either too
much information or too little has been given through the clay
medium.

Product is very poorly organized and there is strong evidence of
3 confusion about the idea or concept. There may be either a large
2 number of unrelated parts or almost no parts available.

Product shows no organizational ability; concept or idea is totally
1 confused or completely lost in the disorganized appearance of the
clay, or may not be present at all.

EXPRESSIVE QUALITIES

In analyzing the product for this aspect, it is important to concentrate on the personal expression the child has been able to make
through the medium of clay. Although the surface of the clay may
have been treated, the spacial qualities extended, and the concept presented with a high degree of organizational ability, the
piece may still lack another ingredient: the child's own personal
touch. Does the product give the impression that the statement
made is unique and fresh, or is it instead stereotyped and dull?

Score

The product indicates that a strong, personal statement has been
7 made through the clay medium. The approach suggests willingness
6 to go beyond the task or assignment and invent, discover and experiment. The expressive qualities, however, work with and support the total clay piece, not in themselves assuming the focus of
the piece.

Product indicates that there was an attempt to make a personal
6 statement through the clay medium. Some willingness to go beyond
5 a task and invent, discover and experiment are present, but the
expressive qualities and the concept are not completely unified.

Product indicates that the statement made goes very little beyond
4 the requirements for the task. Only a minimal amount of originality or imagination are present, and the concept seems somewhat
stereotyped.

Product indicates that the statement made does not go beyond the
3 requirements for the task. No originality or imagination are present,
2 and the final piece seems stereotyped and typical.

Product indicates no personal statement has been made; there is no
1 evidence that the child tried to express anything through the clay
medium.

CLAY UTILIZATION

In analyzing the product for this aspect, it is important to concentrate on the way in which the child has used the medium of
clay itself. Does the plasticity, the forming quality of the medium,
become part of the total work? Does the product indicate that the
unique characteristics of the clay medium were utilized and developed?

Score

The product indicates that the clay medium has been fully utilized
7 and developed. The plasticity and forming qualities of the clay work
6 together with the concept being presented, giving the impression
that the one completely supports the other.

The product indicates that the clay medium has to some extent been
6 utilized and developed. The plasticity and forming qualities of the
5 clay at least partly work together with the concept being presented,
although the one does not completely support the other.

The product indicates that the medium of clay was utilized and
4 developed but only to a limited degree. There is little evidence of
the exploration of the unique characteristics of clay.

The product indicates that the child misunderstood the qualities of
3 clay: he attempted to use it in an unclaylike manner, such as draw-
2 ing with it. The clay medium and the concept do not seem to belong together.

The product does not indicate that the clay was utilized to any
1 extent at all. No exploration of the characteristics of clay seems
evident.

RECORDING SHEET FOR INDIVIDUAL SCORES:

Evaluator _____

SCULPTURAL SCALE

AREA	OVERALL							I SURFACE TREATMENT							II SCULPTURAL SPACE							III UNITY							IV EXPRESSION							V CLAY UTILIZATION							VI AWERAGE						
INDIVIDUAL SCORES	1	2	3	4	5	6	7	1	2	3	4	5	6	7	1	2	3	4	5	6	7	1	2	3	4	5	6	7	1	2	3	4	5	6	7	1	2	3	4	5	6	7	1	2	3	4	5	6	7
NAME																																																	
TOTAL																																																	
NAME																																																	
TOTAL																																																	
NAME																																																	
TOTAL																																																	
NAME																																																	
TOTAL																																																	
NAME																																																	
TOTAL																																																	

RECORDING SHEET FOR CHANGE SCORES:
SCULPTURAL SCALE

Evaluator _____

AREA	OVERALL							I SURFACE TREATMENT							II SCULPTURAL SPACE							III UNITY							IV EXPRESSION							V CLAY UTILIZATION							VI AVERAGE						
Change	-3	-2	-1	0	1	2	3	-3	-2	-1	0	1	2	3	-3	-2	-1	0	1	2	3	-3	-2	-1	0	1	2	3	-3	-2	-1	0	1	2	3	-3	-2	-1	0	1	2	3	-3	-2	-1	0	1	2	3
NAME																																																	
TOTAL																																																	
NAME																																																	
TOTAL																																																	
NAME																																																	
TOTAL																																																	
NAME																																																	
TOTAL																																																	
NAME																																																	
TOTAL																																																	

CLAY VERBS TEST

This test is described in
Chapter Two; findings are
discussed in Chapter Four.

(Please underline circle correct information in all
sections of this form requiring selection
of one answer from several possibilities.)

PRE-INTERVENTION   POST-INTERVENTION

FREE   [PERSON]   DOG

DRAWING

Name of Child _____   Intervention Group:
                                              1. Control   4. Discussion
Computer Number _____   2. Enrichment A
                                              3. Enrichment B   5. Technique
Sex: M___ F___

Ethnic Group: 1 2 3 4 5   Date of Test_____
                                                       Yr.   Mo.   Da.
School _____
                  Number (   )   Date of Birth_____
School Cluster Number _____   Yr.   Mo.   Da.

Teacher _____   Age: Years_____   Months_____
                  Number (   )
                                         Total Months _____
Evaluator _____
                  Number (   )   Grade: Pre-Kindergarten   Kindergarten

                        Time: Begin _____   End _____ = TOTAL _____

PART I

PROCESS EVALUATION

A. In this section, a sequential record of the process used by the child as he engages
    in the drawing is to be written by the evaluator.

    1.

    2.

    3.

    4.

    5.

    6.

7.

8.

9.

10.

11.

12.

13.

14.

B 1 <u>Verbal Activities of the Child: Please check appropriate boxes</u>. R = Related to Clay
NR = Not related to Clay

	R	NR	O
4. Talked almost the entire time while doing drawing without the evaluator talking to him.			
3. Talked alot on his own while doing drawing but worked quietly part of the time.			
2. Talked only when spoken to by evaluator or very little on his own while doing drawing.			
1. Did not talk at all even when evaluator asked questions (child might have used body movements such as shaking head instead of words.)			
B2 1. Talked or sang to the drawing while working.			

C. Please check appropriate box that most closely fits the child's method of doing drawing.

+ 0

	+	0
1. Concentrated on bottom of paper; did not seem to see entire paper as surface to be used in drawing.		
2. Concentrated on edges of paper; did not seem to see entire paper as surface to be used in drawing.		
3. Concentrated on corner(s) of the paper; did not seem to see entire paper as surface to be used in drawing.		
4. Concentrated on center of the paper; did not seem to see entire paper as surface to be used in drawing.		
5. Used entire surface of the paper; seemed to see whole sheet as surface to be used in drawing.		
6. Drew main part(s) of picture only; did not include background.		
7. Drew main part(s) of picture first, then did some background.		
8. Drew background first, then did main part(s) (foreground).		
9. Drew background and main part(s) (foreground) together (did not seem to see them as separate).		
10. Did not attempt to draw; scribbled over paper and stopped.		

D. Child's Feelings About the Drawing: Check number for each item which best suits child's feelings about drawing. Do not score until child is finished with drawing because child's feeling may change during process.

	7	6	5	4	3	2	1
1. Enjoyment: Child seemed to enjoy (owned intimately by child) the act of drawing; he was confident, relaxed, able to concentrate, involved with the act of creating.							
2. Spontaneity: Child did not appear to be trying to please the adult or simply fulfill an assignment; he became involved in the process of drawing to the extent that he was able to let his own feelings and ideas evolve in a free and open manner.							
3. Satisfaction: Child was pleased with his drawing; he expressed his satisfaction by his verbal or facial expressions.							

PRODUCT EVALUATICN

A. Recognizability:

Compare this product with the drawings in the recognizability scale. Decide
which of the ten categories most nearly resembles the product; circle number.

Low 1 2 3 4 5 6 7 8 9 10 High

B. Physical Details:

After child finishes his product, look at it and attempt to identify as many
details as possible; give these a plus. If some details are not clear enough
for you to identify, ask the child what the detail is by pointing to it and
asking, "What is this?" In the appropriate box next to the detail that you
asked the child about, indicate that you did ask him the question, and score the
detail a plus if he identified it; a 0 if he did not, or if he says the detail is
nothing. Don't ask the child to describe or tell you about his product in a
general way.

	tester asked child	+	0		tester asked child	+	0
1. head/body comb.				31. hands			
2. head				32. fingers			
3. body				33. elbows			
4. eyes				34. shape of eye			
5. mouth				35. shape of nose			
6. lips				36. shape of ears			
7. nose				37. shape of hands(paws)			
8. chin				38. shape of body			
9. ears				39. shape of feet			
10. hair				40. shape of mouth			
11. neck				41. style of hair			
12. eyebrows				42. correct number of fingers			
13. eyelashes				43. correct number of legs			
14. eyelids				44. correct number of feet			
15. pupil of eye				45. mustache or whiskers			
16. nostrils				46. beard			
17. teeth				47. penis(child's word sub.)			
18. tongue				48. tail			
19. shoulders				49.			
20. stomach				50.			
21. waist				51.			
22. hips				52.			
23. legs				53.			
24. feet				54.			
25. ankles				55.			
26. toes				56.			
27. toenails				57.			
28. knees				58.			
29. arms				59			
30. wrist				60.			

TOTAL _____

C. Number of Decorative Details: (See instructions for Physical Details)

	asked	+	0		asked	+	0		asked	+	0
1. hair ribbon				15. belt				29. necklace			
2. jacket				16. collar				30. earrings			
3. coat				17. sleeves				31.			
4. hat				18. necktie				32.			
5. dress				19. stripes as design				33.			
6. skirt				20. flowers as design				34.			
7. shirt or blouse				21. decoration on hat				35.			
8. watch				22. cuffs on sleeves				36.			
9. ring				23. buckle				37.			
10. glasses				24. shoelaces				38.			
11. buttons				25. suspenders				39.			
12. shoes				26. purse (held)				40.			
13. socks				27. umbrella (held)				41.			
14. pocket				28. heel on shoe				42.			

TOTAL _____

D. Number of Background Details: (See instructions for Physical Details)

	asked	+	0		asked	+	0		asked	+	0
1. chair				7.				13.			
2. bed				8.				14.			
3. t.v.				9.				15.			
4. house				10.				16.			
5. car				11.				17.			
6.				12.				18.			

TOTAL _____

Total of number of physical details _____
Total of number of decorative details _____
Total of number of background details _____
                                Total _____

E. Correctly Placed Physical Details: Please mark each of the following according to your judgment. + (Plus) means detail is placed correctly; 0 (Zero) means detail is missing or not placed correc

	+	0
1. head on top of body		
2. head on top of neck		
3. arms joined to body		
4. arms joined to body at shoulders		
5. legs joined to bottom of body		
6. eyes placed about halfway down head		
7. nose is halfway between eyes and mouth		
8. mouth is halfway between nose and chin		
9. ears halfway down each side of head		
10. hand at end of arm		
11. fingers appear at bottom of hand		
12. knees about halfway down each leg		
13. feet appear at bottom of legs		
14. toes appear at end of feet		
15. hair on head		

TOTAL _____

F. Proportions:

Before filling out the boxes below, indicate on a scale of 1-10 how in your judgment this child understood proportions of a person, or how well he was able to relate the various parts of a person as regards size to each other.

Low   1   2   3   4   5   6   7   8   9   10   High

Check the number in each section which corresponds most with the product being evaluated.

Body to head

4. Body is larger than head	
3. Body and head are the same size	
2. Body is smaller than head	
1. Not attempted or part missing	

Legs to body

4. Legs longer than body	
3. Legs and body are same size	
2. Legs shorter than body or much longer	
1. Not attempted or part missing	

Arms to body

4. Arms longer than body	
3. Arms and body same size	
2. Arms shorter than body or much longer	
1. Not attempted or part missing	

Eyes to head

4. Eye(s) 1/4 size of head or smaller	
3. Eye(s) between 1/4 and 1/2 size of head	
2. Eye(s) 1/2 size of head or larger	
1. Not attempted or part missing	

TOTAL _____

G. Perspective:

Check the description which best describes the product being evaluated.

7. Figure or shape was drawn so that all of it clearly looks rounded; not just an outline. or outline filled in.	
6. Figure or shape was drawn so that most of it clearly looks rounded; not just an outline. or outline filled in.	
5. Figure or shape was drawn so that a few details clearly look rounded; not just an outline. or outline filled in.	
4. Figure or shape was drawn as an outline only. or outline filled in.	
3. Figure or shape not drawn as a definite form; scribble organization used.	
2. Figure or shape not organized at all; random, unconnected shapes.	
1. Child would not draw a person.	

TOTAL_____

```
                    Total Correctly Placed Physical Details_____
                    Total Score Proportions              _____
                    Total Score Perspective              _____

                                           Total      _____
```

H. Size of Drawing:

Height of figure or total organized product as measured from
top, including background if any, to bottom; use height of
highest completed part(s) if parts were never assembled and/or
scribbled.

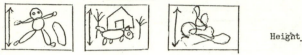

Height_____

Width of figure or total organized product as measured from
widest point; or use width of the same part above used to
measure height if parts were never assembled and/or scribbled.

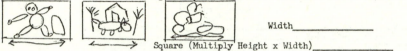

Width_____

Square (Multiply Height x Width)_____

PART III

TECHNIQUE EVALUATION

A. Overall Technique Evaluation:

After reading through the process used by the child and looking at the product,
if any, of the child, try to form a judgment of how well you think the child
understood and controlled the medium of drawing. In other words, did the
child seem to realize drawing has its own unique characteristics and that by
utilizing these, expression through the drawing medium is possible? The
less well the child did in this area the lower his number score; the better
he did the higher his number score. Please circle the number you believe
comes the closest.

        Low 1   2   3   4   5   6   7   8   9   10   High

B. TEXTURES:

The child's use of textures involves any attempt made to show how a
surface or material might feel or look. Textures can be made with
the pencil in a variety of ways; the side of the pencil could be
used to create a filled-in area that is soft and fuzzy looking,
smooth, wavy, etc.; the point of the pencil could be used to create
a bumpy, rough or dotted area; other textures could be made to
indicate a line type of texture: weaves, patterns, etc.

In order to score accurately, it must be clear that the texturing
attempts were deliberate, not accidental. In scoring, check those
items listed (add others if needed) that did have texture. If you
know how the child used the pencil to make the texture, indicate
this in the space provided.

	+	0	How child used pencil to make texture:
1. hair			
2. eyebrows			
3. mustache or whiskers			
4. beard			
5. jacket			
6. coat			
7. hat			
8. dress			
9. skirt			
10. shirt or blouse			
11. shoes			
12. socks			
13. belt			
14. necktie			
15. collar			
16.			
17.			
18.			
19.			
20.			

Total Number of Textures _____

(Please circle correct information in all
sections of this form requiring selection
of one answer from several possibilities.)

PRE-INTERVENTION   POST-INTERVENTION

FREE   PERSON   DOG

DRAWING

Name of Child _____   Intervention Group:
                                            1. Control   4. Discussion
Computer Number _____   2. Enrichment A
                                            3. Enrichment B 5. Technique
Sex: M___ F___

Ethnic Group: 1 2 3 4 5   Date of Test_____
                                                  Yr.   Mo.   Da.
School _____
              Number (   )   Date of Birth_____
School Cluster Number _____   Yr.   Mo.   Da.

Teacher _____   Age: Years_____   Months_____
                  Number (   )
                                         Total Months _____
Evaluator _____
                  Number (   )   Grade: Pre-Kindergarten   Kindergarten

                        Time: Begin _____   End _____ = TOTAL ____

PART I

PROCESS EVALUATION

A. In this section, a sequential record of the process used by the child as he engages
    in the drawing is to be written by the evaluator.

    1.

    2.

    3.

    4.

    5.

    6.

7.

8.

9.

10.

11.

12.

13.

14.

B:1 <u>Verbal Activities of the Child: Please check appropriate boxes.</u> R = Related to Clay
NR = Not related to Clay

	+		O
	R	NR	
4. Talked almost the entire time while doing drawing without the evaluator talking to him.			
3. Talked alot on his own while doing drawing but worked quietly part of the time.			
2. Talked only when spoken to by evaluator or very little on his own while doing drawing.			
1. Did not talk at all even when evaluator asked questions (child might have used body movements such as shaking head instead of words.)			

B2

1. Talked or sang to the drawing while working.

C. Please check appropriate box that most closely fits the child's method of doing drawing.

+   O

	+	O
1. Concentrated on bottom of paper; did not seem to see entire paper as surface to be used in drawing.		
2. Concentrated on edges of paper; did not seem to see entire paper as surface to be used in drawing.		
3. Concentrated on corner(s) of the paper; did not seem to see entire paper as surface to be used in drawing.		
4. Concentrated on center of the paper; did not seem to see entire paper as surface to be used in drawing.		
5. Used entire surface of the paper; seemed to see whole sheet as surface to be used in drawing.		
6. Drew main part(s) of picture only; did not include background.		
7. Drew main part(s) of picture first, then did some background.		
8. Drew background first, then did main part(s) (foreground).		
9. Drew background and main part(s) (foreground) together (did not seem to see them as separate).		
10. Did not attempt to draw; scribbled over paper and stopped.		

D. Child's Feelings About the Drawing: Check number for each item which best suits child's feelings about drawing. Do not score until child is finished with drawing because child's feeling may change during process.

	7	6	5	4	3	2	1
1. Enjoyment: Child seemed to enjoy (owned intimately by child) the act of drawing; he was confident, relaxed, able to concentrate, involved with the act of creating.							
2. Spontaneity: Child did not appear to be trying to please the adult or simply fulfill an assignment; he became involved in the process of drawing to the extent that he was able to let his own feelings and ideas evolve in a free and open manner.							
3. Satisfaction: Child was pleased with his drawing; he expressed his satisfaction by his verbal or facial expressions.							

PART II

PRODUCT EVALUATION

A. Recognizability:

Compare this product with the photographs in the recognizability scale. Decide which of the ten categories most nearly resembles the product; circle number.

Low 1 2 3 4 5 6 7 8 9 10 High

B. Physical Details:

After child finishes his product, look at it and attempt to identify as many details as possible; give these a plus. If some details are not clear enough for you to identify, ask the child what the detail is by pointing to it and asking "What is this?" In the appropriate box next to the detail that you asked the child about, indicate that you did ask him the question, and score the detail a plus if he identified it; a 0 if he did not, or if he says the detail is "nothing." Don't ask the child to describe or tell you about his product in a general way.

	tester asked child	+	0		tester asked child	+	0
1. head/body comb.				31. hands			
2. head				32. fingers			
3. body				33. elbows			
4. eyes				34. shape of eye			
5. mouth				35. shape of nose			
6. lips				36. shape of ears			
7. nose				37. shape of hands (paws)			
8. chin				38. shape of body			
9. ears				39. shape of feet			
10. hair				40. shape of mouth			
11. neck				41. style of hair			
12. eyebrows				42. correct number of fingers			
13. eyelashes				43. correct number of legs			
14. eyelids				44. correct number of feet			
15. pupil of eye				45. mustache or whiskers			
16. nostrils				46. beard			
17. teeth				47. penis (child's word sub.)			
18. tongue				48. belly button			
19. shoulders				49. tail			
20. stomach				50.			
21. waist				51.			
22. hips				52.			
23. legs				53.			
24. feet				54.			
25. ankles				55.			
26. toes				56.			
27. toenails				57.			
28. knees				58.			
29. arms				59			
30. wrist				60.			

TOTAL _____

C. Number of Decorative Details (See instructions for physical details).

	asked	+	O			asked	+	O
1. collar					9.			
2. leash					10.			
3. chain					11.			
4. bone (attached)					12.			
5. toy (attached)					13.			
6.					14.			
7.					15.			
8.					16.			

TOTAL _____

D. Number of Background Details (See instructions for physical details).

	asked	+	O			asked	+	O
1. dog house					9.			
2. bone					10.			
3. bowl or dish					11.			
4. fence					12.			
5. bed					13.			
6. blanket					14.			
7. rug					15.			
8. toy					16.			

TOTAL _____

Total of number of physical details _____
Total of number of decorative details _____
Total of number of background details _____

TOTAL _____

E. Correctly Placed Physical Details: Please mark each of the following according to your judgment: + (plus) means the detail is placed correctly; O (zero) means the detail is not placed correctly or is missing.

	+	O
1. head on top front end of body		
2. head on top of neck		
3. eyes placed on head		
4. nose between eyes and mouth		
5. mouth below nose		
6. ears on sides or top of head		
7. legs joined to body beneath or at lower sides		
8. feet or paws at ends of legs		
9. toes or claws at ends of feet.		
10. tail at back of body		

TOTAL _____

F. Proportions:

Before filling out the boxes below, indicate on a scale of 1-10 how in your judgment this child understood proportions of a dog, or how well he was able to relate the various parts of a dog as regards size to each other.

Low 1 2 3 4 5 6 7 8 9 10 High

Check the number in each section which corresponds most with the product being evaluated.

Body to head

4. Body is larger than head.	
3. Body and head are the same size.	
2. Body is smaller than head.	
1. Not attempted or part missing.	

Eye(s) to head

4. Eye(s) 1/4 size of head or smaller.	
3. Eye(s) between 1/4 and 1/2 size of head.	
2. Eye(s) 1/2 size of head or larger.	
1. Not attempted or part missing.	

TOTAL _____

G. Perspective:

Check the description which best describes the product being evaluated.

7. Figure or shape was drawn so that all of it clearly looks rounded; not just an outline. or outline filled in.	
6. Figure or shape was drawn so that most of it clearly looks rounded; not just an outline. or outline filled in.	
5. Figure or shape was drawn so that a few details clearly look rounded; not just an outline. or outline filled in.	
4. Figure or shape was drawn as an outline only. or outline filled in,	
3. Figure or shape not drawn as a definite form; scribble organization used.	
2. Figure or shape not organized at all; random, unconnected shapes.	
1. Child would not draw a dog.	

TOTAL_____

Total Correctly Placed Physical Details_____
Total Score Proportions   _____
Total Score Perspective   _____

                                 Total   _____

H. Size of Drawing:

Height of figure or total organized product as measured from
top, including background if any, to bottom; use height of
highest completed part(s) if parts were never assembled and/or
scribbled.

                  Height_____

Width of figure or total organized product as measured from
widest point; or use width of the same part above used to
measure height if parts were never assembled and/or scribbled.

                      Width_____

                 Square (Multiply Height x Width)_____

PART III

TECHNIQUE EVALUATION

A. Overall Technique Evaluation:

After reading through the process used by the child and looking at the product,
if any, of the child, try to form a judgment of how well you think the child
understood and controlled the medium of drawing. In other words, did the
child seem to realize drawing has its own unique characteristics and that by
utilizing these, expression through the drawing medium is possible? The
less well the child did in this area the lower his number score; the better
he did the higher his number score. Please circle the number you believe
comes the closest.

            Low 1   2   3   4   5   6   7   8   9   10   High

B. TEXTURES:

>The child's use of textures involves any attempt made to show how a
>surface or material might feel or look. Textures can be made with
>the pencil in a variety of ways; the side of the pencil could be
>used to create a filled-in area that is soft and fuzzy looking,
>smooth, wavy, etc.; the point of the pencil could be used to create
>a bumpy, rough or dotted area; other textures could be made to
>indicate a line type of texture: weaves, patterns, etc.
>
>In order to score accurately, it must be clear that the texturing
>attempts were deliberate, not accidental. In scoring, check those
>items listed (add others if needed) that did have texture. If you
>know how the child used the pencil to make the texture, indicate
>this in the space provided.

	+	0	How child used pencil to make texture:
1. hair			
2. eyebrows			
3. mustache or whiskers			
4. beard			
5. jacket			
6. coat			
7. hat			
8. dress			
9. skirt			
10. shirt or blouse			
11. shoes			
12. socks			
13. belt			
14. necktie			
15. collar			
16.			
17.			
18.			
19.			
20.			

Total Number of Textures _____

DRAWING OBSERVATION SCALE

This scale is described in Chapter Two; findings are discussed in Chapter Four.

(CIRCLE CORRECT INFORMATION)

CLAY   VERBS   TEST

PRE-INTERVENTION   POST-INTERVENTION

Name of Child _____

Computer Number _____

Sex: M ___   F ___

Ethnic Group: 1 2 3 4 5

School _____
                    Number (   )

School Cluster Number _____

Teacher _____
                    Number (   )

Evaluator _____
                    Number (   )

Intervention Group:
    1. Control   4. Discussion
    2. Enrichment A
    3. Enrichment B   5. Technique

Date of Test _____
                  Yr.   Mo.   Da.

Date of Birth _____
                  Yr.   Mo.   Da.

Age: Years _____   Months _____

Total Months _____

Grade: Pre-Kindergarten   Kindergarten

Directions: Use two blocks of clay somewhat rectangular in shape. Ask the child to do
             with the clay what he hears you say as you read the following statements. If
             the child does not understand the directions, read the statement again, but if
             the child still does not know what he is being asked to do, go on to the next
             verbal statement. Mark a plus (+) for those verbal statements the child under-
             stands; a minus (-) for those he does not. Use back of form for any comments.
             (Have clay tools available.)

☐   1. Roll the clay.

☐   2. Squeeze the clay.

☐   3. Pinch the clay.

☐   4. Pull the clay.

☐   5. Flatten the clay.

☐   6. Press the clay.

☐   7. Fold the clay.

☐   8. Take away some clay.

☐   9. Build the clay higher.

☐   10. Draw in the clay.

☐   11. Remove some clay.

☐   12. Smooth the clay.

☐   13. Shorten the clay.

☐   14. Join the clay.

☐   15. Form a point with the clay.

☐   16. Add to the clay.

☐   17. Carve the clay.

☐   18. Lengthen the clay.

☐   19. Texturize the clay.

TOTAL _____

VERBAL ENUMERATION TEST
(DUPLICATES)

This test is described in
Chapter Two; findings are
discussed in Chapter Four.

VERBAL ENUMERATION OF
PERSON OR DOG

ADMINISTRATION

Five (5) minute time limit.

SAY: Tell me the parts of a person (dog) and what a person (dog) has —
like eyes, head, or hat (collar). I will write them on this paper and
we'll make a long list. Now, tell me the parts of a person (dog) and
what he has.
(If the child stops, encourage him or her).

SAY: You know lots of things. Tell me more.
(Wait. Give only one more encouragement. Stop if child does not
proceed.)

STOP AT FIVE MINUTES.

NOTE: If the child starts to respond with a sentence:

SAY: No, just tell me the parts of a person (dog) and what a person
(dog) has.

(If child persists with sentences, allow him to continue and record what
he says. If the child repeats items list these too. Write everything the
child says.)

250

VERBAL ENUMERATION: PERSON / DOG (CIRCLE)

PRE-INTERVENTION   POST-INTERVENTION

Name of Child _____   Intervention Group:
                                        1. Control   4. Discussion
Computer Number _____   2. Enrichment A
                                        3. Enrichment B   5. Technique
Sex: M ___ F ____

Ethnic Group: 1 2 3 4 5   Date of Test _____
                                                   Yr.   Mo.   Da.
School _____
                 Number (   )   Date of Birth _____
                                                   Yr.   Mo.   Da.
School Cluster Number _____
                                        Age: Years _____ Months _____
Teacher _____
                 Number (   )   Total Months _____

Evaluator _____   Grade: Pre-Kindergarten   Kindergarten
                 Number (   )

Directions: On the lines below write the child's responses. (Time Limit - 5 Minutes)

        1. _____   18. _____   35. _____

        2. _____   19. _____   36. _____

        3. _____   20. _____   37. _____

        4. _____   21. _____   38. _____

        5. _____   22. _____   39. _____

        6. _____   23. _____   40. _____

        7. _____   24. _____   41. _____

        8. _____   25. _____   42. _____

        9. _____   26. _____   43. _____

       10. _____   27. _____   44. _____

       11. _____   28. _____   45. _____

       12. _____   29. _____   46. _____

       13. _____   30. _____   47. _____

       14. _____   31. _____   48. _____

       15. _____   32. _____   49. _____

       16. _____   33. _____   50. _____

       17. _____   34. _____   51. _____

USE BACK IF YOU NEED MORE SPACE:

PHOTOGRAPHS OF YOUNG CHILDREN'S CLAY PRODUCTS

Figure One: Range of Young Children's Clay Products: Person

Figure Two: Range of Young Children's Clay Products: Dog

Figure Three: A Child's Clay Person: Pre and Posttest Results

Figure Four: A Child's Clay Dog: Pre and Posttest Results

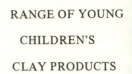

FIGURE 1

RANGE OF YOUNG

CHILDREN'S

CLAY PRODUCTS

PERSON

First Grade

Second Grade

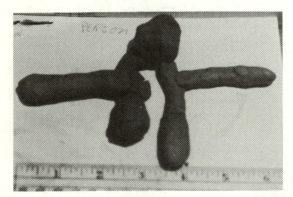

Prekindergarten

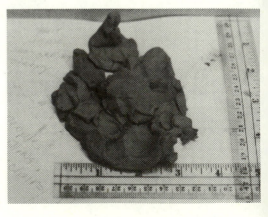

Kindergarten

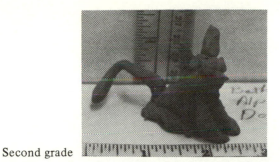

Second grade

FIGURE 2

RANGE OF YOUNG

CHILDREN'S

CLAY PRODUCTS

DOG

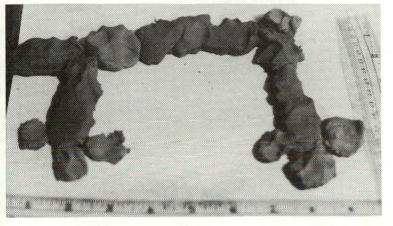

Kindergarten

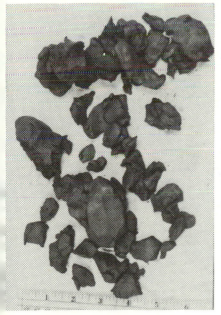

Prekindergarten

Kindergarten

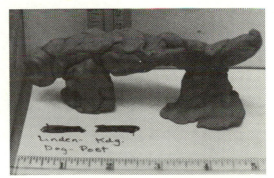

FIGURE THREE

A CHILD'S CLAY PERSON: PRE AND POSTTEST RESULTS

Pretest Person

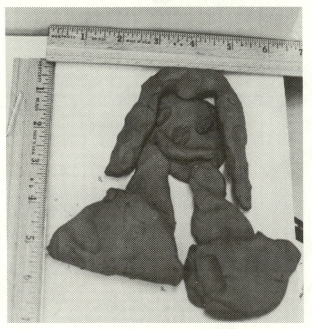

Posttest Person

FIGURE FOUR

A CHILD'S CLAY DOG: PRE AND POSTTEST RESULTS

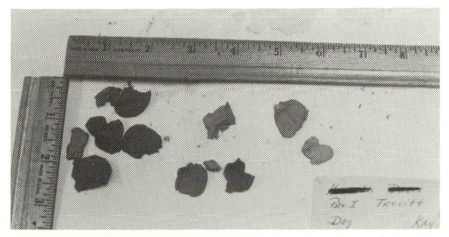

Pretest Dog

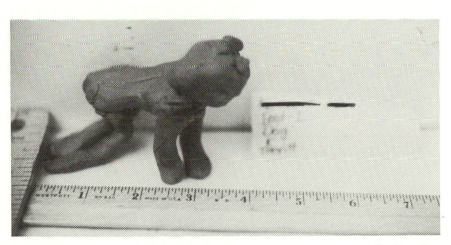

Posttest Dog

SUGGESTED REFERENCES

Baratz, Joan C., "Linguistic and Cultural Factors in Teaching Reading to Ghetto Children," in *Remedial Reading: Classroom and Clinic*, Schell and Burns (Eds.). New York: Allyn and Bacon, 1972.

Bender, L., and A.C. Woltman, "The Use of Plastic Material as a Psychiatric Approach to Emotional Problems in Children," *American Journal of Orthopsychiatry*, 1937, 7, 283–300.

Bernstein, Basil, "Social Class, Linguistic Codes and Grammatical Elements," *Language and Speech*, 1962, 5, 221–240.

Broudy, Harry S., "Arts Education: Necessary or Just Nice," *Phi Delta Kappan*, January, 1979, 5, p. 349.

Brown, Eleese Virgin, *Developmental Characteristics of Clay Figures Made by Children from Age Three Through Age Eleven.* Illinois State University: ERIC Document Service, 71–21802 501025, 1971.

Cherry, Clare, *Creative Art For The Developing Child.* Belmont, Calif.: David S. Lake Publishing Co., 1972.

Deutsch, Martin and Martin Whiteman, "Social Disadvantage as Related to Intellectual and Language Development," in *Social Class, Race and Psychological Development*, ed. by M. Deutsch, Irwin Katz, and Arthur Jensen. New York: Holt, Rinehart and Winston, 1968.

Eisner, Elliot W., *Educating Artistic Vision.* New York: Macmillan, 1972.

Fantani, Mario D. and Gerald Weinstein, "Making Contact with the Disadvantaged," in *Radical School Reform*, Gross (Ed.). New York: Simon and Schuster, 1969, p. 173.

Garritson, Jane Schmalholz, *Child Arts: Integrating Curriculum Through the Arts.* Menlo Park, Calif.: Addison-Wesley Publishing Co., 1979.

Goldstein, Bernard, *Low Income Youth in Urban Areas: A Critical Review of the Literature.* New York: Holt, Rinehart and Winston, 1967.

Golomb, Claire, *Young Children's Sculpture and Drawing.* Cambridge, Mass.: Harvard University Press, 1974.

Hagan, Judith C., "The Sculptural Analysis of Clay Products Made by Children Ages 4–8." Unpublished Master's Thesis, The Ohio State University, 1977.

Harris, Dale B., *Children's Drawing as Measures of Intellectual Maturity.* New York: Harcourt, Brace and World, Inc., 1963.

Hartley, R.E., et al., *Understanding Children's Play.* New York: Columbia University Press, 1964.

Hawkinson, John, *A Ball of Clay.* Chicago: Albert Whitman Co., 1974.

Holt, John C., *How Children Learn.* Pitman Publishing Co., 1969.

259

King, Martha L., "Language: Insights from Acquisition." *Theory Into Practice.* December 1975, 5, p. 296.

Langstaff, Nancy and Adelaide Sproul, *Exploring with Clay*. Washington, D.C.: Association for Childhood Education International, 1979.

Lewis, P. Helen, et al., *Improving Verbal Cognitive Skills of Disadvantaged Preschool Children Through the Arts*. Title III Project Termination Report, Columbus Ohio. May, 1977. ERIC Documents #ED 161 536.

Lowenfeld, Victor, *Creative and Mental Growth*. New York: The MacMillan Co., 1970.

Mooney, Ross L. and Sara Smilansky, *An Experiment in the Use of Drawing to Promote Cognitive Development in Disadvantaged Preschool Children in Israel and the United States*. Washington, D.C.: U.S. Department of Health, Education and Welfare, Office of Education. September, 1973.

Nelson, Glenn C. *Ceramics: A Potter's Handbook*, sec. ed.. New York: Holt, Rinehart and Winston, 1966.

Piaget, Jean, *Science of Education and the Psychology of the Child*. New York: Orion Press, 1976.

Position Paper for the Association for Childhood Education International (1976) quoted by Ira J. Gordon, "On the Continuity of Development," *Childhood Education*, January 1976, p. 126.

Post, Henry and Michael McTwigan, *Clay Play: Learning Games for Children*. Englewood Cliffs, New Jersey: Prentice-Hall, Inc., 1973.

Rosen, Connie and Harold. *The Language of Primary School Children*. New York: Penguin Books, 1973.

Smilansky, Sara and T. Boaz, "Advancing Language and Cognitive Performance of Young Children by Means of Earth-Clay Modeling," in *The First Ten Years of Life*, ed by M.L. Hemes, I.J. Gordon, and W.F. Breivogel. Gainesville, Fla.: Division of Continuing Education, University of Florida, 1976.

– – –, *An Experiment to Examine the Possibility of Advancing the Cognitive Level of Disadvantaged Kindergarten Children by Means of Clay-Modeling*. Szold National Research Institute of Research in the Behavioral Sciences, Jerusalem, 1972. (In Hebrew and English translations.)

– – –, *An Experiment to Examine Possibilities of Advancing the Cognitive Performance of Young Children by Means of Earth-Clay Modeling*. Publication of NIE, Department of Health, Education and Welfare, Washington, D.C., October, 1977.

Warren, Kenneth S., M.D., and John T. Bruer, Ph.D. *Memorandum To: Student Counselors, Medical School Deans of Admission*. New York: The Rockefeller Foundation, 1981.

Wollheim, Richard, *On Art and the Mind*. Cambridge, Mass.: Harvard University Press, 1974.

LIST OF TABLES

263

INDEX

265

topics
　　for intervention, 40, 57—58
　　selection of, 57, 58
transfer
　　of learning, 19, 30—31, 78, 89, 95,
　　99, 101, 105, 110
　　limitations of, 31
twenty-first century, challenge of, 12,
　　175

United States clay study, 35

validity, 19, 38, 47
verbal development, 86
verbal skills, 26

Wechsler Pre-school and Primary Scale
　　of Intelligence (WPPSI) 48, 96—99
　　(see TESTS)
wedging clay, 135
Weinstein, 26
Wollheim, Richard, 23
workshops (see TEACHER TRAIN-
　　ING)
work-time, 137

The Authors:

Sara Smilansky, PhD
> Professor of Child Clincal Psychology and Education, Department of
> Psychology, University of Tel-Aviv, Israel

Judith Hagan, MA
> Coordinator, School for the Visual Arts, Columbus Public Schools,
> Columbus, Ohio

P. Helen Lewis, PhD
> Assistant Professor of Education, Indiana University at South Bend

For further information:
> School systems, colleges and universities, PTA's and other groups of inter-
> ested people who may wish to have a seminar or workshop on *Clay in the
> Classroom* may write to the address below. Video tapes, slide presentations,
> packaged materials, workbooks, and hands-on activities are available, with the
> presence of one of the Clay Project staff members to conduct the seminar or
> workshop. Costs and formats vary according to the amount of time and
> materials required, and will be adjusted if a group purchases sufficient copies
> of the *Clay in the Classroom* text.

Write to:

Judith Hagan, Coordinator
School for the Visual Arts
546 Jack Gibbs Blvd.
Columbus, Ohio 43215

(614) 464-4591

or   Dr. Helen Lewis
1002 S. 20th St.
South Bend, Ind. 46615

(219) 287-6830